Praise for *Min*

"Regardless of what you think you ~~~~~~~~~~~~~~~~~~~~~~~~~~~ ial advice, when you look at them through a lens of mindfulness, they look different. Clearer. Less charged. Jonathan DeYoe systematically describes the why and how of investing, weaving stories and activities throughout this engaging book. He urges us to invest in our happiness and appreciate the wisdom of being boring investors rather than chasing the next new shiny thing."
— **Mary Martin, PhD**, author of *Mindfulness for Financial Advisors*

"*Mindful Investing* teaches you how to take your emotions out of the investment process and how to be more logical and plan-driven with your financial decision-making. The book is an interesting, easy, and enjoyable read. I highly recommend it."
— **Tom Corley, CPA, CFP**, author of the Rich Habits series

"Rediscover the role that money plays — not only in building wealth but, more importantly, in building a life based on purpose and intention. Jonathan DeYoe brilliantly articulates how to connect the dots between our financial habits, emotions, belief systems, needs, and choices — and how these factors influence the very fabric of our financial future. This book is about more than money; it's about investing in yourself and the search for your own definition of freedom."
— **Ron Carson**, founder and CEO of Carson Group

"For anyone who feels overwhelmed or anxious at the thought of investing, Jonathan DeYoe has written a brilliant book to guide you to simplicity in your finances. These pages are filled with decades of wisdom from someone who is a master at mindfully managing money."
— **Adam Carroll**, founder of The Shred Method™

"Jonathan DeYoe's first book, *Mindful Money*, offered readers an easy path to a personal financial plan, and in *Mindful Investing*, he shares how to get the most profit from your portfolio with the least amount of time and effort. Great investment insights."
— **Jim Britt**, ten-time #1 internationally bestselling author of the Cracking the Rich Code series

"The remedy for emotional investing is mindful investing. Jonathan DeYoe has developed a practical and actionable strategy for finding success as an investor."

— **George Grombacher**, financial adviser
and author of *Be Your Own CFO*

"Whether you know a lot or a little about investing, *Mindful Investing* is an insightful read on why and how to invest. The 'mindfulness' nuggets cast a calm veil over what can be a stressful topic. Money is not about hoarding but about growing and compounding a sliver of your earnings to create a life in accord with your values, wishes, and goals. The thoughtful exercises, proven investment strategy, and motivating quotes provide a road map to a secure and confident financial future. With history, philosophy, and research-based investment methods, Jonathan DeYoe arms you with the tools to meet your financial goals."

— **Barbara A. Friedberg**, CEO of Wealth Media and editor of
Personal Finance: An Encyclopedia of Modern Money Management

"This book makes investing so much easier than you can imagine! I've worked in the money and investing business for nearly thirty years and have never read such a succinct and easy-to-understand investing manual. This is the book I'll be recommending from now on. Thank you, Jonathan, for giving away your secrets and making it simple for readers to get busy investing."

— **Leisa Peterson**, author of *The Mindful Millionaire*

"*Mindful Investing* is a breath of fresh air when it comes to investing. Jonathan DeYoe's honest and straightforward approach serves as a how-to guide for both new and seasoned investors. In its pages, you will get an investing strategy that is time-tested, thorough, and gentle all at the same time. I loved this book and will recommend it to friends, family, and clients alike!"

— **Holly Morphew**, founder and CFO of Financial Impact
and author of *Simple Wealth*

Mindful
Investing

Also by Jonathan K. DeYoe

*Mindful Money: Simple Practices for Reaching
Your Financial Goals and Increasing Your Happiness Dividend*

Mindful Investing

RIGHT FOCUS,
BETTER OUTCOME,
GREATER WELL-BEING

Jonathan K. DeYoe, AIF

Foreword by Robert Seawright

New World Library
Novato, California

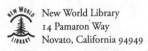 New World Library
14 Pamaron Way
Novato, California 94949

Text design by Tona Pearce Myers

Library of Congress Cataloging-in-Publication data is available.

First printing, September 2023
ISBN 978-1-60868-876-0
Ebook ISBN 978-1-60868-877-7
Printed in Canada on 100% postconsumer-waste recycled paper

 New World Library is proud to be a Gold Certified Environmentally Responsible Publisher. Publisher certification awarded by Green Press Initiative.

10   9   8   7   6   5   4   3   2   1

For my brother's sons, Evan and Asher.

I place this book in your hands with three hopes:

1. that you are surprised.
2. that you can appreciate it one day.
3. that you can embrace this method the same way your father did before you, as it will save you many headaches.

Contents

Part 1: Why We Invest

Part 2: How to Invest

Foreword

Almost twenty-five years ago, Christopher Chabris and Daniel Simons created one of psychology's most famous experiments, sometimes cheekily called "gorillas in our midst." Subjects are told that they will watch a one-minute video of two teams of three passing basketballs to one another. The subjects are instructed to count the number of passes made by the team wearing white shirts.

The first time I saw the video, I (correctly!) counted the passes but, like roughly half of all test subjects, entirely missed the person in a gorilla suit who pranced into the experiment, stopped to beat his chest, and then sauntered off screen. I was so focused on counting passes, I missed pretty much everything else.

This experiment has two obvious interpretations: (1) we miss a lot of what goes on around us; and (2) we have no idea that we are missing so much. We think we see ourselves and the world as they really are, but instead, we often see the world as *we* really are. We see what we want or expect to see and miss a lot.

When I was in law school, I officiated youth basketball games to supplement my financial aid package. I had refereed a lot previously, but never so consistently and never semi-professionally. Once I had gotten the basics down (e.g., knowledge and application of the rules, authority, positioning, demeanor, etc.), I was surprised at what I realized was my most consistent weakness and problem as an official: I tended to call what I expected to happen rather than what did happen. I'm sure it occurred more often than I recognized, but I recognized it far too often for comfort, even when I ultimately made the correct call.

As I saw plays develop, I frequently thought I knew what was going to happen, based on lots of previous experience. For example, an awkward reach-in leads to a foul. Sometimes what I expected to happen didn't happen. Still, I whistled according to what I expected to happen far too often. I had to fight that tendency constantly. My expectations colored my judgment and even (I'm sure, based on plenty of good research studies) my perception. I "saw" what I expected to see.

In other words, I missed the gorilla. We all suffer from that tendency at least some of the time.

But the implications of the invisible gorilla aren't all bad. What we look for goes a long way toward determining what we see, it's true. However, other research has shown that mindfulness increases the accuracy of our perception. This excellent book will help you with that.

More importantly, this book provides helpful guidance directed at where and how we place our attention. If what we are looking for matters so much, we need to be looking for and focusing on the right things to be successful. *Mindful Investing* will help you do exactly that — gorillas or not. I hope you will appreciate it as much as I did.

— Robert Seawright,
chief investment officer at Madison Avenue Securities, LLC,
and founder and writer of *The Better Letter*

Introduction

To achieve great things, two things are needed:
a plan, and not quite enough time.
— Leonard Bernstein

They say that ignorance is bliss. In the world of investing, however, ignorance — especially when partnered with fear — is the biggest predictor of failure. Once we conquer both ignorance and fear, financial stability and success can be ours. Even bliss if we're lucky.

One of the most important factors in individuals' financial success is their own behavior. Our emotions can play a huge role in our decision-making processes, and once we're mindful of this we can make better choices. We may start out our journey merely ignorant, but all too often fear or greed takes the wheel, steering us toward financial disaster. Mindfulness is a powerful tool, helping us to pause and reflect on what's *really* happening. This allows us to acknowledge our feelings without necessarily *acting* on them, before turning back to the facts at hand. Keep emotion out of your decision-making and stay nonreactive in the face of fear or greed. It's not easy, but it *is* simple.

Human beings tend to make things more complicated than they need to be, particularly in the absence of information.

If all you know about investing comes from the movies, you might well picture a bunch of fat cats in suits scrunching their faces at a ticker tape machine, red-faced and angry or victorious and jubilant. Either way, it looks stressful, and probably beyond the means of the average person. The good news is that's only the story the media tells us. The reality? Investing is simple. It is also boring. But that's a good thing, right? If you're like most of my clients, you're not reading this book because you want to become a stockbroker. You're here because you want to find an easier, less stressful, and — most importantly — more successful and stable way to invest your money so that it will grow steadily and outpace your need for income into retirement and beyond.

The goal of this book is to help you understand how investing works, how to make an investment plan, and how mindfulness plays into the success of that plan. Successful investing doesn't involve secrets, tips, or special expertise. It involves understanding the big picture of how the markets work, particularly understanding that in the long term the market reliably recovers from virtually any challenge. And the key is just that: the long term.

In this book, I not only explain the process of investing but make it simple, enjoyable, and digestible. I'll do that by showing you some real-life examples of how investment tools play out. The goal is to understand:

- what makes you happy and why a plan is important to getting there.
- that investing in the simplest way provides the greatest long-term outcomes.
- what I mean when I say simplify, simplify, simplify!
- why you should start by saving consistently.

- how often you should be looking at your portfolio (hint: rarely).
- when to listen to the media (answer: pretty much never).
- the limitations of your own market knowledge.
- that a long-term outlook is key to your portfolio's success.
- how to take ownership of your story.

Mindful Investing is broken into two parts: *why* we invest and *how* to invest. In part 1, we'll explore the history of investing and both its purpose and its psychology. In part 2, we'll look at how best to begin an investment journey, what types of investment accounts are out there, how to evaluate risk and return, and what type of returns you can expect to see in the short and long term. I'll share how I invest and how to avoid common (and some less common) pitfalls. We'll end by looking at how new investment trends play out in today's world of social media and speculation.

The goal is to first understand how the market works so that you can be blissfully educated, not ignorant. As part of this education, we'll examine common fears about the market (and why they're often unwarranted) as well as how to overcome them through mindfulness. Once we're aware of our emotional reactions to the market's ups and downs, we can practice noticing them as they happen and then mindfully choosing not to react. The secret to investing success is to stop predicting, start planning, and stay mindful so your investments will last your lifetime and beyond.

The entire financial structure of your life should be based on how you define success for yourself, and that starts by looking at what makes you happiest in life. That is a concept we explored in *Mindful Money*, my first book. *Mindful Investing* is all about the next steps: understanding what personal success looks like for you, ignoring the media's noise, making an investment plan that aligns with your goals, and then mindfully sticking with it. That's it! The hardest part is building and maintaining your faith in the market's ability to recover. If you can do that, you can simplify the rest and reap the rewards. The first step toward planning your future is to understand the past, starting with your own history. To provide you an example, I'll start with mine.

PART I

Why We Invest

CHAPTER I

The Tale of the
Nine-Year-Old Investor

All fortune belongs to him who has a contented mind.
— *PANCHATANTRA*

A lot of people ask how a Buddhist like me became a financial adviser. They want to know the relationship between Buddhism and finance — two areas that would appear to be diametrically opposed. And that, to me, is what's so beautiful about it. You take finance, a field many people associate with greed and desire, and you infuse it with one of the core practices in Buddhism: mindfulness. Mindfulness is the nonjudgmental awareness of reality as it presents itself. When this concept is applied to investing, something powerful happens: we realize that investing is incredibly simple and not something we need to give much attention to at all. How so?

1. We first take the time to understand what it is we truly need to make us happy in this life.
2. We create a financial life plan around those happiness goals.

3. We invest according to the plan.
4. And then we can blissfully tune out all the noise as we sit back and earn what I call the happiness dividend — the joy and satisfaction from a life well lived.

The best part is that the smartest investment plan is incredibly simple! And once you've made your plan — and the key here is to *make* that plan — you can spend as little as a couple of hours each year tending to it.

In my twenty-six-and-counting years as a financial adviser, I've learned that before looking to the future and creating a financial plan, it's important to first look back and understand our own history. To do this, we'll briefly look at the history of investing in the United States and how that has shaped where we are today. Then, before diving into all the hows and whys of investing, I'll ask you to look at your own history with the practice, if any, so that you can be mindful of your biases before crafting an investment plan that works for you. I'll go first.

My History

Long before I decided to pursue a master's degree in Buddhist studies, before I practiced daily meditation, before I'd ever heard the word *mindfulness*, I knew I wanted to be involved in finance. I bought my first stock at the age of nine. How does a nine-year-old even think to buy stocks? you might wonder. What was the driving force? Like many things, it started out of want. Growing up, I did not have, so I wanted. That's not to say my brother and I were wearing barrels and eating from tin cans, but we grew up not having all the things that the other kids at school had.

Allow me to back up a little.

Before I was born, my dad was an electrical engineer for

UNIVAC, manufacturers of ENIAC, the first general purpose, electronic, digital computer. We're talking early vacuum tube technology. Computers the size of buildings. And if my family had stayed in Silicon Valley, I'm sure we would have had a drastically different life. Maybe my dad would have raked in the money, and we'd have bought fancy clothes, gone to private schools, had personal tutors, and driven cars that weren't beaters. But my parents wanted to raise their kids in a place where you could always leave your front door unlocked, where children were safe walking to school and had a yard to play in. They also wanted to be sure we learned from an early age the value of working for what we wanted. Thus, right before I came along, my parents packed up and moved to the quiet hometown safety of Rapid City, South Dakota.

While writing this book, I asked my mother about the choice to move, how it affected our lives, and what she thought about my interest in money. In an email, she wrote:

> From the time you were quite young you ALWAYS wanted to have the BEST. Remember the huge aquarium for the piranha? The top-of-the-line camera? The compound bow? Etc., etc. I'm guessing that came from watching what other kids had, but you never verbalized that to us.... You grew up thinking you were poor because we were "poor." I know you were told "we can't afford that" often.... But we also didn't discuss our personal finances with you guys a lot when you were younger because you didn't need to know those difficulties.

I want to pause here to recognize the beautiful thing my parents saw, which it took me a long time to see — that the choice to move to South Dakota was based on a core value far more important than money or social status. My parents wanted their children to grow up safe and happy. They worked their asses off to provide that without exposing us to their financial challenges.

Back to my interest in finance.

Like many children, I didn't realize until many years later how much my parents really sacrificed for my younger brother and me. All I heard was "no" and "we can't afford that" when I asked for new toys or shoes or *things* in general. What I didn't see was how much of their time my parents sacrificed; how they rarely bought new clothes or nice items for themselves; how they drove clunky old cars and worked two jobs each. All so my brother and I could sign up for soccer, get swimming passes at the community pool, go skiing, and do at least some of the fun things that children want to do.

Still I wanted. The kids at school had cool shoes and nice bikes and the latest toys. My best friend had an early Apple computer; I had a Commodore VIC-20. It was hard to see that stuff those kids had and not to want some of it too. But my parents couldn't afford to buy me those things, so I had to find a way to earn enough money to buy them for myself. So I became interested in money. I didn't have any thought of taking care of my family or anything like that. My motivations were simple: I didn't have, so I wanted. Enter my introduction to investing.

A Boy and His Stock

Antoine de Saint-Exupéry, author of *The Little Prince*, famously said that "a goal without a plan is just a wish."[*] This

---

[*]   Dominique V. Turpin, ed., *The Essential Book of Business and Life Quotations* (New York: Anthem Press, 2023), s.v. "goals."

concept is crucial to investment planning. Ideally, you deter-mine your goal, create a plan that will meet that goal, set the plan in motion, and then let it be. Back when I was nine, my goal was to buy a bicycle. I'd heard my dad and his friends talk about the stock market and thought that would be a good way to earn some money for my bike. I started paying closer attention to what my dad was reading in *Money* and *Kiplinger*, and some days when he set the magazines aside I'd pick them up and flip through, trying to gain insights into how I could make some cash. One day when my parents were doing some errands downtown, I slipped into a broker's office and discov-ered the Value Line Investment Survey.

I started reading up on what to buy. With a little per-suasion, I convinced my dad to help me gather my birth-day, Christmas, and lawn-mowing money — a grand sum of $400 — and I made my first investment, in a bank holding company called First Bank Systems.

I'm sure you won't be shocked to hear that nine-year-old me lost most of my money on that stock. The savings and loan crisis exploded and over half my investment vanished. It was a real blow, but I was determined to get that bike. And since I was only nine, my dad ended up paying me back the $200 or so I'd lost, and I recovered pretty quickly. But that first ex-perience with investing whet my appetite. Soon after, my dad pushed me to try again.

I can't say my next investments were wildly successful ei-ther — I was a child, after all — but I *really* wanted money. And thus the salesman in me was born. While I was still in grade school, I started running a little sales empire, selling candy and gum to my classmates and sandwiches door to door to my neighbors. As I got a bit older, I started working with my dad on various business schemes, some more successful than others. For example, one of my dad's least successful endeavors was a button business. He bought a button-making machine, and we produced pins and ribbons that said stuff like "1st Place" or "Good Job," which I'd sell door to door throughout different neighborhoods. Sadly, the people of South Dakota were not ready for our product. The list of jobs continues, and my work-hard-for-the-money mentality carried me through college.

Here, another pause to share a piece of my family history that shaped the type of financial planner and investor I'd eventually become. My dad taught me to invest, but my mom taught me to save. Once I started working all these little sales jobs, my mom would force me to save 50 percent of my income — an idea that I resented at the time, of course, but later thanked her for. Ultimately those savings paid for my college. As a going-to-college gift, my parents split the cost of my first car with me (a $1,200 rusted-out Mazda GLC), but otherwise I was on my own for tuition, books, and room and board. Thus I worked full-time through college as well.

A Will to Wealth

I went to college with a will to wealth. I wanted to be *rich*. But a year and a half into studying finance, I was bored. So I shifted focus and took a semester to study English literature. I read a lot of Shakespeare, but what I *really* fell in love with was philosophy. I set finance aside for a while and went on to complete my undergraduate degree in philosophy and religious studies.

My classics professor, Marvin Shaw, saw how much I enjoyed this work and encouraged me to take my passion to grad school. I applied to the Graduate Theological Union to study as a Lutheran seminarian, but fate had other plans. First, I got a scholarship with a Lutheran seminary, but the institution ended up having to revoke the offer due to lack of funding. I asked other schools if they would support my studies. The Institute of Buddhist Studies agreed to do so if I worked in its library in return, a task I happily took on throughout my time in grad school — which ended up being shorter than I'd planned.

Somewhere around the midpoint of earning that degree, my wife at the time said she wanted to go back to school too. To support her, I ended up dropping out, putting my finance hat back on, and getting a traditional job as a stockbroker at Dean Witter. But as the saying goes, before the sun comes the rain. Or, in my case, a downpour. I started a business that imploded. I got divorced. I weighed in at 290 pounds. I couldn't get enough scotch, pizza, and ice cream (not typically all at the same time, but I'm sure I had my moments).

Bottom line: I was a mess. I had to recalibrate.

A big part of why I was so unhappy during this time was that I wasn't doing what I wanted with my career. That "doing what you love" notion might seem like a no-brainer, but it was incredibly transformative once I realized what I wanted to do and made the switch. I had to learn a lot of hard lessons first, at seven different Wall Street firms; but once I started my own firm, where we really focused on financial education and planning, everything shifted. I could see the ease in my clients' faces when they'd made an investment plan that would help bring them to their happiness goals. There was no longer a fight to keep up with the headlines, no more of that panicked salesman mentality. The firm was goal-oriented and planning-driven, and we succeeded because our clients succeeded. That was the real payoff.

The Pursuit of (Real) Happiness

This chapter in my personal history leads me to the present. It grieves me to share that around the time I started this book, my brother died suddenly. After that incredible loss, my family and I came together in a new way. We started having conversations that we'd never had before. A lot of those were around the stuff of life: What is the meaning? What is *our* meaning? How does money tie into all of this?

My parents and I had some deep and difficult discussions. Up until then, I'd had no *idea* about many of the financial choices and sacrifices they had to make to provide the life they gave us. As a result, I came to a lot of humbling conclusions. What if I'd been given that bike I wanted so badly? I'd never have invested in that first stock. What if I'd been given those shoes, the toys, the car, the college tuition? I'd never have had the pleasure (so to speak) of having to work from grade school through grad school and beyond. I'd probably not have the same work ethic. I'd probably not have studied finance. Or Buddhism.

One question that plagues me today, and which perhaps always will, is that of how much I should give *my* children. How much do I insist that they earn their own money? When do I say no, even if I can afford to say yes? I want my children to know what it's like to work hard for something. I want them to understand that money isn't the driving factor behind happiness. That ultimately money can be a tool to help manifest the things that help *bring* happiness, but most importantly that money management — and, specifically, investing — can be simpler than most people think. More on that later.

Business Meets Buddhism

Back to that beautiful union of Buddhism and finance. As I mention earlier, Buddhism teaches mindfulness, here defined as a nonjudgmental awareness of the present moment as experienced through our senses, thoughts, and feelings. In even simpler terms, mindfulness teaches us to be aware of what is going on in the Now. When I was first pursuing my master's in Buddhist studies, I struggled with the question of how to live in the Now while also planning for my financial future.

What I came to realize was that having a financial plan, which inevitably includes a smart investment strategy, is what affords us the ability to "just sit." How? Once you have your plan in place, you leave it be! Remember the old informercial tagline, "Set it and forget it"? That's not unlike what I'm prescribing: set your plan and, no matter what's going on in the storm around you, forget changing it. Stick nonreactively to your plan, and by the end of your investment journey you *will* come out safe and secure on the other side.

Does Mindfulness Actually Work, Though?

Developing mindfulness isn't just a nice idea. This method has been growing in popularity over the last few decades, and there is plenty of science to back up its effectiveness.

For example, a 2018 Harvard study found that those who practiced mindfulness experienced less stress and were able to think more clearly, which translated to better decision-making and overall happiness.[*] In another study, Harvard researcher Sara Lazar found that regularly practicing mindfulness meditation can change the size of key regions in the brain associated with memory, emotional regulation, perspective-taking, and self-referential processing.[†] We can change our *brains* by

---

[*] MGH Public Affairs, "Mindfulness Meditation and Relaxation Response Affect Brain Differently," *Harvard Gazette*, June 20, 2018.

[†] Sara W. Lazar et al., "Meditation Experience Is Associated with Increased Cortical Thickness," *Neuroreport* 16, no. 17 (2005): 1893–97.

practicing the simple art of mindfulness meditation. That's pretty amazing stuff.

Mindfulness helps us to look at what is going on in our own world without being distracted by all the noise that's happening around us. As applied to our investing choices, mindfulness teaches us to stick with the plan we've set for ourselves. It allows us to pay no mind to the media, predictions of an impending recession or expansion, or the latest recommendations from so-called pundits.

What I meant earlier by "nonjudgmental awareness" is the ability to let go of certain opinions we may experience in reaction to breaking news. Take, for example, the spread of Covid-19. In March 2020 as Covid was first making its way across the land, the markets dropped and panic ensued. People saw the news and said, "Oh my God, this is terrible! It's the end of the world!" — and a whole lot of them reacted by selling their stocks. Those sellers watched this event with judgment; they lost their belief in the potential for the markets to recover.

And recover is exactly what the markets did, only three months later — the fastest recovery in our nation's history. At the end of those three months, the markets were back at their previous highs, which means that those panicked sells were a terrible idea. When current events seem frightening, the most important thing we can do is to sit on our hands and wait for the scary event to pass, confident that the markets will bounce back. So far, every dip in history has been followed by a full recovery, whether we're talking about the Great Depression, the dot-com crash, the subprime mortgage crisis, or the Covid-19 downturn.

Every prediction, no matter who makes it, is a judgment about potential future outcomes. As I write this in 2023, there is a lot of talk about the debt ceiling and the brinkmanship between political parties. Many pundits are predicting a recession. But even though we may agree conceptually with that thesis (or any prediction), it is impossible to make investment policy based on it for the following reasons:

1. We don't know if the thing (in this case, failure to raise or eliminate the debt ceiling) will happen.
2. We don't know *when* it might happen (since they can kick the can down the road in perpetuity).
3. We don't know *how* they will resolve the issue.
4. We don't know *how long* the resolution will take or last.
5. We don't know how capital markets will respond.

If we don't know any of these details, how can we possibly make logical, consistently successful investment decisions in reaction to these issues? We can't.

Enter Mindful Investing

Most of my clients practice what I call *mindful investing*. They make mindful choices about what a happy present and future means for them, create a financial plan around those choices, then stick mindfully and nonreactively to that plan. To use the above example, when the markets crashed in March 2020, those clients stuck mindfully to their investment plans despite the sometimes-overwhelming urge to sell. Instead, they waited patiently (many even added more capital to their investments), and sure enough the markets recovered. I can't emphasize enough how important it is to remember that the markets have always recovered in the past, and there's no reason to believe they won't in the future. Any individual's long-term success is a matter of weathering the storm.

When you make an investment plan and stay mindful of it no matter what, you don't have to worry about any particular variables. The right plan, one that aligns with what you need, frees you from having to pay too much attention to the market's ups and downs or any advice that doesn't align with your plan.

In the next chapter, we're going to look at the history of investing in the United States and how the evolution of investing options and adviser mentalities have influenced what kinds of investment choices we are able to make.

MINDFUL INVESTING ACTIVITY

Each chapter in this book ends with a Mindful Investing Activity. Readers of my first book, *Mindful Money*, may recognize some of them. That's because my key themes are woven throughout both books. If you're starting with this book, the exercises will be new; if you've already read the first book, you'll find yourself refining what you've learned and reinforcing principles and practices. As in the first book, many of these are writing exercises that ask you to put pen to paper and express your thoughts, dreams, feelings, and goals. When I say "put pen to paper," I mean that literally — I highly encourage putting aside the laptop or tablet and taking an old-school, analog approach to the writing exercises. This isn't just a personal preference; there's a lot of science behind it. One joint study between Princeton and UCLA found that when people take notes by hand, they are more likely to remember important information than those who type, a result that's been verified in many further studies.*

The first part of this exercise is the easiest one in the book. Before you do anything else, choose something to write *on* and something to write *with*. Be both creative and practical and choose something that feels right for you. Use a spiral-bound notebook, a hardbound bullet journal, or an old-fashioned yellow legal pad to do every Mindful Investing Activity in the book, and choose a writing implement that feels natural in your hand. A fountain pen virtually sings to me, but you may prefer a No. 2 pencil, a rollerball pen, or a handful of color pencils. Whatever works! Every time you open this book, have your notebook and pen at the ready both so that you're prepared for the exercises, and so that you can jot down notes about things you want to come back to or contemplate further.

The second part of this exercise is harder. Even if you've already done this exercise while reading my first book, do it again from scratch. You've no doubt learned and remembered things that will add nuance and detail to the exercise, and it will be key to setting you up for success in the following chapters.

---

* Pam A. Mueller and Daniel M. Oppenheimer, "The Pen Is Mightier Than the Keyboard: Advantages of Longhand over Laptop Note Taking," *Psychological Science* 25, no. 6 (2014): 1159–68; Umejima Keita, Ibaraki Takuya, Yamazaki Takahiro, and Sakai Kuniyoshi, "Paper Notebooks vs. Mobile Devices: Brain Activation Differences During Memory Retrieval," *Frontiers in Behavioral Neuroscience* 15 (2021): doi .org/10.3389/fnbeh.2021.634158.

On the first page of your notebook, tell your family's financial story in answer to the following prompts. Your answers don't need to be long, but they should tell a story that helps to illuminate the financial truths you live by today (and perhaps some habits you need to reexamine).

- What facts and fictions were you taught about money growing up?
- What habits, both good and bad, did you learn?
- What feelings and fears did you absorb?
- What financial successes and failures did you witness growing up?
- What childhood financial lessons and illusions have you carried into adulthood?

CHAPTER 2

A Brief History of Investing

*The disadvantage of men not knowing the past
is that they do not know the present.*
— G. K. CHESTERTON

A scene in the film *The Wolf of Wall Street* shows Mark
Hanna (played by Matthew McConaughey) sitting down
to lunch with Jordan Belfort (played by Leonardo DiCaprio).
Hanna tells Belfort that it doesn't matter who you are, Warren
Buffett or Jimmy Buffett, no one knows how stocks are going
to perform. It's a big, phony illusion that stockbrokers or any-
one else can know what a stock will do next. It's all "fugazi," as
Hanna proclaims, downing his martini.

Sure, brokers can speculate on which stocks are likely to
go up or down, and sometimes they're right. Sometimes they
buy at the perfect time, and sometimes they sell just in time
too. But "sometimes" is not something you should be trusting
your life savings to. Relying on speculation is one of the most
unstable decisions any investor can make. Investing should
not be a complicated endeavor involving reading the headlines
and reactively moving your money around. As I'll come back

to repeatedly in this book, successful investing is beautifully simple. We'll go more into the simple, stable side of things later, but first I want to address the common worry that financial advisers can't be trusted because "they just want your money." I get it. Things used to be different. Key word: *used* to be. To help demystify what financial advisers do today, let's take a little trip through the halls of history and look at how things used to work.

A Quick History Lesson

Pre-1980s

"Big fat commissions" was the name of the game before the 1980s. There was no internet. Most people only bought US stocks and bonds, there were few companies to choose from, and brokers made significant commissions on every stock they sold. The character Gordon Gekko (played by Michael Douglas) perfectly summed up the attitude in the 1987 movie *Wall Street* when he said, "Greed is good." That's right. Every stockbroker had money on the brain, and not much else.

Brokers charged a fixed rate for all trades, regardless of size. This meant that the market was designed to only be accessible to those with considerable wealth; small investors had to pay hundreds of dollars in fees to invest at all. High-net-worth individuals had *all* the access to the stock market, and big brokers were *still* bleeding them dry. All that came to a screeching halt on May 1, 1975, referred to on Wall Street as May Day, when the Securities and Exchange Commission (SEC) mandated that the brokerage industry deregulate commissions. Trading fees were no longer fixed, but rather set by market competition. In the following decades, this mandate paved the way for the discount brokers we know and love today.

1980s

The deregulation of commissions continued to drastically lower broker fees through the 1980s and into the 1990s. Legacy financial institutions and their greed for high commissions had ignored the types of investors who were now able to take advantage of the wave of discount brokers like Charles Schwab, TD Ameritrade, E*TRADE, and Scottrade (now part of TD Ameritrade), which were making investing accessible to a broader range of people. These companies were seen as a serious threat by the brokers who had gotten used to raking in billions in commissions every year. According to Investopedia, my favorite online investment encyclopedia, some brokers even started referring to the SEC as the "Soviet Economic Committee."* (That's how much they were against changing the commission structure, accustomed as they were to taking their big cuts of all buys and sells.) But as it usually does, change happened anyway. Between 1975 and 2000 the cost of a single stock transaction dropped 90 percent — all thanks to May Day and the rise of discount brokers that followed deregulation.

1990s

The brokers who hated the SEC's mandate found ways to adapt. Instead of selling individual stocks as they had done before the 1980s, they started selling mutual funds, or portfolios of stocks, bonds, and other securities. (For more on mutual funds, check out chapter 9.) Between 1990 and 2000, mutual

---

* Cory Mitchell, "May Day," Investopedia.com, updated April 25, 2022.

fund holdings went from $500 billion to almost $6 trillion —
an increase of *1,100 percent!*

Mutual fund supermarkets were born, and the number
of commission-based mutual funds started to decline. The
first SEC-compliant exchange-traded fund hit the scene. (For
those who wonder what ETFs are, we'll be diving deep into
the topic in chapter 11, when we talk about diversification.)
Schwab, TD Ameritrade, and E*TRADE offered commission-
free (also known as load-waived) funds, and consumers could
read *Kiplinger, Money,* Morningstar, and Yahoo! for advice on
which funds to buy. It's arguable whether this information was
always sound, but its very existence forced product manufacturers and brokers to adapt again.

Instead of offering individual funds, brokers were offering
asset allocations (blends of funds, an important concept that
we'll discuss at length in chapter 9). At first, brokers were still
using the commission model for these sales but soon ditched
that in favor of charging a fee for advice. This in turn meant
that financial guidance became both more sound and more
comprehensive.

The 1990s were also a turning point for financial advisers.
New securities meant advisers could focus on risk management and diversification in a way they never had before. They
could build fully customized portfolios for their clients, tailored to help them address their needs and protect their assets
from inevitable market downturns.

Before we move into the 2000s, I'd like to take a step back
into my own history on Wall Street to share more details on
the ins and outs of how these transactions worked. I started at
the peak of the buy-sell mentality, right before the tech bubble
burst. Commissions were still the name of the game. And I
wouldn't go back to those days even if I could.

What Can I Do to Get You into a Stock Like This Today?

As we've discussed, investing today is much different than it was before. In the '90s, brokers like me were stock pickers, meaning we sold individual stocks and our clients had to trust our advice for two key reasons. First, laypersons weren't able to place trades on their own, so they *had* to have brokers to trade for them. And second, we had access to knowledge and reports that weren't available to the public, and we had colleagues whose job it was to speak directly to the CEO of any company we were interested in. We'd tell our clients what we knew, and they kind of *had* to believe us. If we insisted that a certain stock was a great buy, our clients would often say, "Okay, I trust you." We'd pad our pockets with commissions, the clients *might* make money, and the cycle would continue.

For example, if you were a client of mine in 1996, I would have cold-called you to sell you either Cisco stock or a municipal bond (also known as munis, these tax-free government bonds are typically used to raise money for things like road repairs and school maintenance). If you purchased the Cisco stock, I would then call you back with another blue-chip "growth" idea such as Microsoft, Intel, Advanced Micro Devices, or Oracle. If you were making money on my recommendations, I was building trust with you. Next, based on that trust I would call again to say, "Let's take a look at your total portfolio." If you agreed, we would set a meeting and start working together for real. If you weren't ready yet, I would suggest a more aggressive stock like Juniper Networks or Broadcom. Or if you weren't comfortable with that, we would go back to talking about a muni bond. The process was entirely broker-driven. I would call with an idea, and if the *last* idea I'd called you with had worked you would usually buy the new idea. The more times you bought based on my ideas, the more commission I made, and the closer I was to my goal of managing your total portfolio.

At the same time, I would be cold-calling other prospective clients to talk about muni bonds. If I found someone that was interested, I would sell them the new issue bonds that Morgan Stanley was currently underwriting (these were not commission sales, but I was paid handsomely for selling them regardless). As with stocks, I would call again with a new bond whenever we had one on offer. Eventually, I would ask about their equity portfolio and see if they owned Cisco, Microsoft, Intel, Advanced Micro Devices, or Oracle. If they did, then we would get into the more aggressive options.

It was a security-by-security process. I would build a position with thirty to fifty clients at any one time and call them all frequently to let them know about new research on the stocks they owned. Since laypeople didn't have access to the same data we did, clients had to trust us when we told them that any hot news of the day meant they should buy ABC Company or sell XYZ Company. Part of the Morgan Stanley Dean Witter training for new brokers covered how to convince customers to heed our calls to buy and sell. For better or worse, most of my customers listened.

There would be big commission days when I completed thirty to fifty sell transactions and thirty to fifty buy transactions. By the end of my first year, I had over three hundred customers. The goal was to open as many accounts as you could as quickly as you could. We had scripts to follow: "Oh, you don't own this stock? Why *not*?" "Oh, you own this one already, smart move — you'll want this other one as well then." Picture a used-car salesperson peppering you with any and all reasons why you should absolutely take this particular junker home today.

You know what? It was awful. There was this constant, stress-inducing need to move money around, to convince clients of the next greatest stock. If they made money, fine. And if they lost money, we weren't supposed to care. I almost quit multiple times. Then finally I did.

I left Morgan Stanley Dean Witter for Paine Webber, where the clientele was a little different. I started cold-calling people at their desks at tech companies. I'd set up meetings to help them diversify out of their company stock, manage their taxes, and handle their stock options. I didn't sell stocks ever again; from then on it was always portfolios, which we'll talk in depth about in part 2 of this book. But now it's time to move on to the 2000s.

Early 2000s

As computers became more powerful, financial advisers were able to use turnkey asset management programs (TAMPs) to oversee their clients' investment accounts while they focused on other areas of their business. TAMPs took care of "back office" tasks like account administration, billing, and portfolio allocation. In return, advisers had more time to seek out new clients, strengthen existing relationships, and help all of them tackle their financial goals. Advisers became asset gatherers.

And then the 2008 financial crisis struck. It was a dark time for the US economy. Housing prices fell by 33 percent. Unemployment skyrocketed to over 9 percent. People lost their homes and retirement savings. The financial industry had to adapt.

2010s

The 2007–8 housing collapse gave birth to a new tech-driven industry that disrupted financial services once again.

Robo-advisers like Wealthfront and Betterment hit the scene in 2008 and gained popularity through the 2010s. By the end of 2020 close to a hundred high-tech, mostly automated investing platforms were available to investors of all backgrounds.

2020s and Beyond

Financial advisers have been, are now, and will continue to be reinventing themselves. One new frontier is the rise of the registered investment adviser (RIA). An RIA is not just committed but legally obligated to always act in the best interest of the client. RIAs charge a fee for advice and do not make commissions on sales. They tend to focus on planning and behavioral advice, helping clients to explore their goals, understand the trade-offs, and know what they need to do to make *their* dreams come true — and then support them in doing it. The Vanguard Group, Morningstar, Russell Investments, and others praise the power of behavioral advice. And advisers have begun to adopt these new service requirements as a way to keep earning their fees (and the trust of their clients). In chapter 7 we'll go into much more detail on how financial advisers can help you, and when it might be a good choice to hire an adviser as a one-time consultant or for a long-term partnership.

Another trend we're seeing, particularly among younger investors, is a growing interest in what's known as environmental, social, and governance (ESG) investing with funds that focus on issues related to climate change and sustainability. For some, this is one component of mindful investing: deliberately investing in funds that champion causes that are important to the investor, regardless of whether they're the most financially lucrative option. Younger clients are also less likely to use actively managed funds — which, as the name implies, are actively managed by a human being and thus tend to have higher fees with no guarantee of higher rewards. Portfolio managers are just people and people are fallible. Instead, the next generation of investors has embraced passive fund management, meaning there is no manager actively buying and selling funds and trying to beat the market. Passively managed funds have lower fees and higher long-term success rates. More on that later.

As in any industry, if you can't beat 'em, join 'em. A financial adviser that can't adapt to the changing needs of our financial atmosphere will disappear, either by selling to firms that are adapting or by being slowly fee-compressed into oblivion.

The next frontier of financial advice will be personal transformation, with the adviser becoming one part finance professional and one part behaviorist. Speaking with the perspective of decades of experience, hundreds of clients served, and millions of dollars managed, I can say that every poor investment decision is a behavior problem, not an investment problem. Sound financial planning requires two equally important parts: making a financial plan and *sticking* to it. You may find that a vital part of your individual success is partnering with a financial adviser who will help you to mindfully stay with that plan you made when the world wasn't crumbling and the pundits weren't screaming. A good adviser will remind you of historical trends and help you avoid panicking no matter what's happening in the world (and thus the markets).

Yes, there will be zigs and zags in the market, but long-term investment planning requires you to sit mindfully and resist making any decisions based on your biases and fears. You'll find this to be a relief — you get to ignore pundits urging you to buy cryptocurrency or invest in NFTs. When the markets dip, you get to ignore the fear that you'll lose it all.

Why? How? Because, while an individual company may fail, the markets have always recovered and there's no reason to believe they won't continue to do so in the future. We can reassure ourselves of this by looking at history. Before we move forward, let's take a moment to examine yours.

MINDFUL INVESTING ACTIVITY

The goal by the end of this book is for you to create an investment plan that aligns with your happiness goals. The first step in creating that plan involves two things:

1. reflecting on what you need in this life to make you happy, now and into retirement.
2. recognizing your existing investment beliefs and being open to changing them.

Regarding the first, in *Mindful Money* we looked in depth at what I call the pillars of happiness, so I won't do that again here. That said, it's important to recognize that the specific things you need, particularly in regard to retirement, are not going to come about by magic. Sure, some of us were graced with silver spoons, but most of us must face the harsh reality that unless we mindfully plan for retirement our golden years will be less than dazzling. In chapter 12 we'll go more in depth on how to create your investing plan, so hold that thought for now.

Reflecting on the second component, it may be helpful to look back at the family history you wrote in chapter 1's exercise. With all of this in mind, ask yourself the following questions:

- What do you know about how investing works?
- What are your investing beliefs?
- Do stocks seem terrifying?
- What does your portfolio look like? Or do you not have one yet?
- Is there a financial guru you trust? If so, why?
- What was the biggest investing mistake you've ever made?

I encourage you to pause and consider these questions before moving forward. If it's helpful, write your own history with investing so you can keep that "learning from history" mentality in mind as we go along. Once you've had some time with that, we're going to answer the question "What *is* investing anyway?"

CHAPTER 3

What *Is* Investing Anyway?

Wealth unused might as well not exist.
— AESOP

L et's start with the most basic of answers to that question, the *Merriam-Webster* definitions of the verb "to invest":

1. To commit (money) to earn a financial return.
2. To make use of for future benefits or advantages.
3. To involve or engage, especially emotionally.

Many people worry that investing is too risky. Just the word itself inspires anxiety in some. But it's important to foster a positive relationship with the word and its various implications. As we've already touched on, part of that "too risky" misconception stems from watching decades of the all-too-common buy-sell mentality play out. People have earned a lot of money in stocks, but people have lost quite a bit too.

So here is what's *actually* risky:

1. Not investing at all.
2. Buying individual stocks.

In later chapters we'll go into all sorts of details on what I mean when I say "buying individual stocks," but for now keep in mind the concept of diversification (another concept we'll explore more deeply as well). The easiest way to understand diversification is that it's the very definition of not putting all your eggs in one basket. The best way to do this is by buying broadly diversified ETFs* or funds,† which — sticking with the egg analogy — is like buying multiple eggs in multiple baskets. The key is to be so diversified that if one stock goes down you won't lose so much money that you regret being born.

Risky item number one might sound counterintuitive. How could *not* investing be the riskiest financial decision you can make? To answer this, it's important to understand the concept of risk as it applies to financial decisions, as well as the impact of inflation on our overall financial health.

Why *Not* Investing Is What's Risky

Something I ask my clients all the time is why they would want to have a fixed income portfolio in a world of rising costs. Like everybody else these days, we're talking about inflation. To start our exploration of this concept, let's look at some preconceived notions investors may have, based on years of watching how chaotic the stock market appears and all the lives it has built or crushed.

---

* An ETF, or an exchange-traded fund, is a basket of securities that is traded on the stock market. ETFs are a way to stay broadly diversified. More on that later.

† For example, an index fund, which is a fund structured to match a certain market, such as the S&P 500. Index funds can be made up of one hundred, five hundred, three thousand, or more tiny slivers of different stocks — so a downturn in any one company won't affect your overall portfolio's success. More on this later too.

First, there are two ways of thinking that we need to dispel:

1. The belief that bonds are the safe way to go. This feels true in the short term but doesn't tend to be true long term. While bonds are not as volatile as stocks, they have a hard time keeping up with inflation over time.
2. The belief that stocks are inherently risky. Again, this feels true in the short term, but the goal here is to keep your eye on the long-term patterns. Stocks are volatile, but they do the best job of maintaining "purchasing power" (i.e., keeping up with and defeating inflation) over time.

Each of these beliefs stems from the misconception that money and currency are the same thing. In fact, *currency* refers to the amount of dollars someone might have, while *money* more broadly refers to the value of those dollars in terms of the goods and services they can purchase. Here's the thing: the value of currency is always declining because of inflation. The real risk, when thinking about one's retirement income, *should* be seen as the declining value of that income due to inflation, which translates into reduced purchasing power.

Here's an analogy I often use to explain inflation and purchasing power to my clients. I ask them, "Okay, what did a slice of pizza cost when you were, say, twenty-five years old?" For this example's sake, let's say this was in the year 1980 and you were in New York City, where that slice would cost you sixty cents. Today, let's say that same slice of pizza from Di Fara in Brooklyn is five dollars. Same delicious pizza, same relative cost to other consumer goods of the time. But if you were to save a dollar bill from 1980 and present it to your pizzeria in the year 2023 expecting to get forty cents change, they'd say, "Cough up the other four bucks, friend." Same dollar bill, different buying ability over time.

What Is What: Investing and Assets

So we return to the question "What *is* investing, really?" Simply put, investing is the act of putting money into something with the expectation that you'll earn that money back and more. I like the definition at the top of this chapter that includes "to make use of for future benefits or advantages." Investing, whether it's in ourselves, our businesses, or our portfolios, is something we should intend to continue over a period of ten, twenty, thirty, forty years, and counting.

When I think about investing, I think about *businesses*. In portfolio terms, the most common investment tool we think of is stocks, which are tiny portions of a business. When the business does well, their stockholders do well too.

Before moving into the nitty-gritty of *how* to invest and looking at all the investment tools and strategies out there, I want to go over a few of the most crucial concepts to understand as we move through this portion of the book. For further and more detailed definitions, you really can't beat the online investment dictionary Investopedia.

Let's start by talking about assets, which are any resources that you own that have economic value. There are three main asset classes: stocks, bonds, and cash or cash equivalents (which means any account that can be liquified and usable immediately, for example, money market funds, certificates of deposit, or short-term government bonds). Each of these types of assets has very different risk/return characteristics.

Cash Is Cash

Cash can be physical cash (notes, coins), checking or savings accounts, or money market funds — currency that can be exchanged immediately for the purchase of goods (say, pizza) or services (say, your electricity bill). Clients often ask how much cash they should have on hand, and how much to tie up in investments. The answer is different for each person, depending on your age, but generally speaking I recommend having enough cash on hand for at least three months of living expenses, but no more than two years' worth (after that, you're much better off investing rather than continuing to save for a potentially rainy day). We'll go into more detail on that in chapter 6 when we talk about how to get your accounts in good shape *before* you invest,* but for now the most important thing to keep in mind about cash is this: cash is a liquid asset, meaning it is available for immediate use but is not necessarily making you money.

Cash is important to have on hand for expenses, of course (mortgage or rent, bills, all the stuff you *do* in life), but if you think that adding cash to a straight-up savings account will keep you safe into retirement, you are sorely mistaken. Thanks to inflation, that sixty cents you saved for pizza is not going to buy you more than some crust twenty years from now.

To help illustrate what we're talking about, figure 1 (see next page) shows how a savings account would grow over a thirty-year period if it were opened with a $100,000 deposit. Using an average interest rate of 0.06 percent, by the end of its first year of savings it would have made a return of $60. Using that same 0.06 percent interest rate, by the end of thirty years that account would have grown to $101,816. You may be able to get a higher return on your savings right now, but inflation is also running a lot higher these days. It isn't the precise number that matters, whether we're talking about earnings or

---

* Chapter 22 of *Mindful Money*, "Build an Emergency Fund," goes into more detail on how much cash to have on hand at different stages of life.

inflation, but the *relationship* between those numbers. Over extended periods, inflation will always overwhelm savings.

The second column demonstrates how inflation increases the cost of goods over that same thirty-year period. Using the long-term inflation rate of 3.1 percent, the cost of goods and services over thirty years would rise from $100,000 to a whopping $249,896. Even after one year, the dollars required to purchase the same basket of goods and services would rise by $3,100 — meaning that after a year the account holder would already be significantly behind. Simply put, a savings account will *not* keep up with inflation. Your assets must grow faster than your spending.

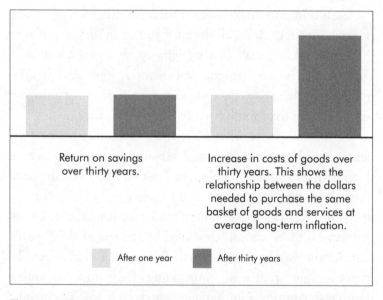

Figure 1. Return on savings versus increase in cost of goods over thirty years

We're going to continue exploring this vital concept throughout the book, but keep in mind the key point that saving *without* investing will not keep up with inflation and will not make your income last in retirement. That is, unless you're one of the lucky few who has buckets of cash that'll last you for the rest of your life — but even if you had millions, why would you let that money sit idly when it could be making money for you, your family, and whatever legacy it is you want to leave behind?

Bonds, a Source of Fixed Income

The most important thing to know about bonds is that they are another source of fixed income. Bonds offer a set regular income and a guaranteed return of principal at the end of a specified period.* In some ways, that guarantee can be a good thing; high-quality bonds are a lot less volatile than stocks, which means that you aren't losing any money if the market takes a dip. However, bond yields are not as high as market returns, and this difference compounds over time.

A bond is a lending instrument. As mentioned before, tax-free municipal bonds are issued by a state or local government and are typically used for repairs or maintenance on things like schools, roads, and sewage systems; they are not taxed by the federal government or by the state in which they are issued. You can buy a muni bond that matures soon (a couple of months) or in the distant future (a few decades).

Say you buy a short-term muni bond in the amount of

---

* A bond is guaranteed by whatever entity issues it, but not all guarantees are the same — some are strong and some are weak. For example, a federal Treasury bond is backed by the full faith and credit of the US government. That's a strong guarantee. However, if you bought a bond from, say, a brick-and-mortar VHS rental store, you might not see your interest payments or principal back. That would be a weak guarantee.

$1,000. Maybe the terms are three years with 0.3 percent yield to maturity. That means you would receive three dollars per year in tax-free interest, and at the end of that three years you'd receive the return of your $1,000 principal. That is a fixed income asset, because that $1,000 is guaranteed by the issuer of the bond.

Why do bonds exist? When a company or government entity wants to borrow money, they can go to a bank and take out a loan, but sometimes it's cheaper for them to hire an investment bank to create a bond and sell it to the public. When a member of the public buys the bond, they are lending the company money. So that $1,000 bond is not FDIC insured, but it's guaranteed by the borrowing entity (the company or municipality that issued it). There will be a set interest rate and a fixed end point (the maturity date) for when that bond will be paid back in its entirety.

To reiterate, bonds are lending instruments. The company borrows the money to invest in, say, its equipment, infrastructure, and hiring or other processes. In exchange, the company promises you a fixed interest rate and maturity date.

The most important thing to note here is that bonds provide a fixed income. And if you'll recall one of my favorite maxims, why would you want a fixed income in a rising-cost world? You don't. Or at least you shouldn't if you want your income to keep up with your rising costs well into retirement.

The only portfolio asset that is *not* fixed? Stocks.

Equity, Stocks, and Shares

In *Wall Street*, Bud Fox (played by Charlie Sheen) comes up with a scheme to buy BlueStar, the failing airline company that his father works for. He convinces all his broker friends to have their clients buy up as much BlueStar as they can, then they collectively dump the stock all at once so that the share value plummets precipitously. At that moment, Fox's new billionaire investment friend, Sir Larry Wildman (played by Terence Stamp), can swoop in and buy up all the available BlueStar stock. He does so, becomes the company's primary shareholder, and thus is able to save the airline while making big bucks.

To back up for a moment, stocks, equities, shares — all these terms refer to the small slivers that you can purchase of a publicly traded company. When we invest in stocks, the "stock" is a piece of paper (or now the digital version of that), while the investment is in a share of the business itself. For example, if you own one share of Apple, you own a tiny slice of the company. You are investing in Apple's future, with good faith that the company will continue to grow. A single share is a minuscule percentage of the company, and that gives you the right to that percentage of the growth and dividends Apple pays in perpetuity. As long as you own that slice of the Apple pie, so to speak, you'll receive dividends from the company's growth over time. When we talk about investing in stocks, we're really talking about investing in businesses, one sliver at a time.

Of course, you have the option to sell that share at any time; and as with any transaction, the buyer receives the seller's shares, and the seller receives the buyer's cash payment. As the seller, you receive the then-current price of the share sold (which is hopefully more than you paid for it, meaning you'd see a profit). The buyer of that share then receives all future growth and dividends in Apple, forever. There is *huge* value in that forever thing. As long as Apple is in existence, as long as it's paying a dividend and growing, and as long as you own that share, you make money too.

Conversely, if you were banking, so to speak, on those dividends from Apple to offer a big payout and it were to go under, as a partial owner you'd lose all the money you'd invested in them too. Which brings me back to one of the most important ideas in this whole book: *owning a single stock is a bad idea.* Unless you're a big investor like Sir Larry Wildman from *Wall Street,* you are not going to be able to own enough shares of any one company to rely on its success to bring *you* success. And conversely, if you did lose a bunch of money from a stock purchase that plummeted, you wouldn't lose your whole fortune, and you'd still be fine. If you were wealthy like Wildman, you could afford that type of risk. Most of us regular folks don't have a billion, million, or even hundred thousand bucks to play with. We must instead make smart, safe, long-term choices with our money if we want to earn enough to carry us into old age.

So What Is Mindful Investing?

We've lightly defined investing, but what do I mean when I say *mindful* investing? When you apply the concept of mindfulness — the nonjudgmental awareness of reality as it presents itself — to investing, there are two vital pieces:

1. Mindfully looking at what you really need to make you happy (both now and in the long term), then making an investment plan to match your needs.
2. Once you've done that, avoiding the noise.

A key concept in Taoist philosophy is *wu-wei,* or intentional nonaction. Doing without doing. I love this concept when applied to investing: once we've determined what we need and made a plan around that financial need, we get to do nothing.

The key is to *do* the planning part;* but once you've determined the amount of money you'll need, which includes the right amount of savings and the right amount of time and patience (while staying broadly diversified and regularly rebalancing),† you are freed from the market timing and investment selection judgments that other people have to make. Patient nonaction fosters serenity, stillness, and trust. Make a plan, then *wu-wei*.

It doesn't matter what the investment tools are; the issue is the humans who are employing them. As a financial adviser, one of my primary goals is to help manage my clients' behavior. There's something in our being that wants to sell dramatically when the markets are going bear (falling significantly) or buy drastically when the markets are bull (rising significantly). The challenge is to sit patiently with the plan we made and not react to the current environment; in other words, to trust in the process.

There are three distinct challenges to being a human investor. First, in most cases, we don't know what we are doing. There is *no* practical education about money anywhere in our lives (unless we seek it out). Even if we did know something useful, the knowledge is rarely accessible when we need it.

Second, there is way too much bad information out there, ranging from foolish lies (told by people writing about market history, economics, or how business works who don't know any better) to motivated lies (told by those who want to sell us something because their commissions or clicks depend on

---

* We'll get to investment planning later in this book, but for more detail, see my first book, *Mindful Money*, which really gets into the whys and hows of making an overall financial plan. In this book, we'll do a much lighter version of that process.

† Rebalancing is something we'll get detailed with in chapter 12, but for now know that it means periodically buying or selling assets to realign your portfolio with your planned asset allocation.

our listening to them). The lies compete for attention with the boring truths that force us to make trade-offs, sit still through anxiety, stay humble in the face of the things we cannot know, remain patient when every fiber of our being is telling us to take action (*any* action), and be disciplined about following the plan we knew worked in one of our more enlightened moments (before all the emotions took hold).

Finally, we must contend with our cognitive and emotional biases, many of which can be played on by both the foolish and the motivated lies.

One last note on investing brings us back to the third part of that definition that we started this chapter with: "to involve or engage, especially emotionally." To me, this speaks to one of the most important investments you can make — in yourself.

You Are Your Most Important Investment

Warren Buffett said, "The best investment you can make is an investment in yourself.... The more you learn, the more you'll earn."* Investing in your own financial education should be a simple, ongoing process. For some reason, few high schools offer practical courses like money management and investing. Teenagers become adults at the age of eighteen and go out into the world with little to no education about the importance of saving and investing or the nuts and bolts of how to do so.

Aside from investment learning itself, *you* are one of the most important things you can invest in. That could mean continuing your education in some way to work on your craft or investing in your own idea to start a business. In fact, owning a business is one of the smartest (albeit most difficult) investments you can make.

---

*   Tyler Gray, "Warren Buffett Gives Financial Advice to 10-Year-Olds," *Fast Company*, April 4, 2013.

Take my friend Gary Ray. Gary was passionate about gaming and, after doing plenty of research, he reached out to initial investors (me included) who believed in his idea to open a store. Gary's business model was sound — a game store that offered regular tournaments and game nights — and his passion was obvious. We couldn't *know* that Gary would be successful because no one can predict anything, but we knew that he had a damn good shot. Opening Black Diamond Games was how Gary invested in himself. And now he gets to live a life that suits him. He's not a millionaire — nor does he want to be — but he makes what he needs to be happy. Gary determined what would bring him happiness on the day-to-day, figured out a way to make enough money to support that, then created an investment opportunity that would benefit himself and those around him. We'll revisit Gary's story in chapter 13.

MINDFUL INVESTING ACTIVITY

What types of investments have you made in yourself? And perhaps most excitingly, what types of investments *will* you make in yourself? Is there a creative project, a new skill, or a business idea you've had in the back of your mind for years? Perhaps someone you know is interested in opening their business and you can be involved by investing in them.

Write down the investment you want to make in yourself, whatever it is. Now think about what steps you can take toward that goal. You're on your way to a plan!

Let's continue the conversation about why investing is important by exploring what it can do for you, your family, and your community.

CHAPTER 4

The Purpose of Investing

Understanding human needs is
half the job of meeting them.
— ADLAI STEVENSON

Y ou may be familiar with Maslow's hierarchy of needs, which is a theory of motivation that says there are five basic levels of human need that dictate our behavior.[*] The bottom rungs of that pyramid are the basics: food, shelter, safety. These form the foundation for what humans need to be "okay" before being able to reach the things toward the top of the pyramid (e.g., love and belonging, esteem, self-actualization).

Similarly, the purpose behind investing can be broken down into three key categories: security, responsibility, and legacy. Security is what I always wanted to build as a kid. My dad's business failed when I was three, and my family didn't have a regular income until I was in high school. For this reason, I put security — a sense of personal security (basic okayness) — as the first and most basic benefit of investing.

---

[*] Nicole Celestine, "Abraham Maslow, His Theory and Contribution to Psychology," PositivePsychology.com, September 29, 2017.

Security, Part 1: Lifestyle

Of course, we want the basics beyond the basics — those life *things* that give us momentary joy and add up to our personal definition of success: to live in a place we like, to dine out, to subscribe to our favorite streaming services, to travel, et cetera. Of course, each of us has a slightly different list of these things. What's important is to home in on what makes you most happy, to allow yourself to spend appropriately on those happiness-inducing things, and to limit spending in areas that do not add to your happiness. Not everyone's needs are the same, so it's important to determine yours.*

For me, a huge goal with investing is the invaluable gift of time — to eventually have the freedom to spend my time how I want to spend it and to not have to do what other people tell me to do. To reach this goal means not only having a stable source of income, but also allocating that income smartly between savings and safe long-term investments. Thanks to that very real thing called inflation, savings alone will *not* get you there. You must invest.

Security, Part 2: Retirement

As a kid, I heard a lot about this thing called retirement. I didn't understand the concept, but I knew that it was a goal at some point. In *Mindful Money*, we talked about how the first thing most people should think about in financial planning is retirement — maybe that's true for you and maybe it's not. This idea of what's most important, of course, comes from a very personal place. For me, retirement is the other, equally important part of

---

*　This is what *Mindful Money* is largely about: determining your "pillars of happiness" and then making a financial plan around those happiness factors.

financial security. We don't want to have to work forever. Eventually, your mind and body will give out. And maybe at some point, regardless, you just won't *want* to keep working.

My uncle Dick was a truck driver. As I write this, he is eighty-two years old. He retired from truck driving at the age of eighty. He worked his entire life because he couldn't save enough. Before becoming a truck driver, Uncle Dick had been a rancher for many years. When he lost the ranch in the 1970s, he had a lot of financial responsibilities to take care of for himself and his kids; by the time he was in his sixties, Social Security was far from enough to cover those expenses. He started driving a truck for a living. Here's the thing about my uncle Dick: he never asked for money from anyone else. It was important for him to support himself because he knew he still could. He lives a humble life and it's all by his own doing. Uncle Dick is a great example of somebody who took responsibility and made the hard choice to keep working. He knew he didn't have enough savings because of circumstances in his life, so he worked. That's the reality for a lot of people.

There are countless stories of people who work into their eighties and nineties. Some of them do so because they want to (maybe they're passionate about their work; maybe they're saving to leave that big legacy behind), and some because they *have* to. But what about jobs that are physically taxing? Construction workers make decent money, but few people can maintain such a physical job forever. Then of course there's the idea that most of us don't *want* to keep working.

Each of us pictures something different when we think of retirement. Maybe you see yourself relaxing on the porch with a glass of iced tea, golfing, enjoying the grandkids, gardening during the day, and playing canasta at night. Or maybe you envision traveling the world.

Regardless, most of us want to be able to stop working at some point. It's an inescapable truth that one day we will all rely on our saved and invested resources for an income stream. Whether we outlive that income is dependent on two things:

1. Saving enough
2. Investing

The average retirement age in the United States has been sixty-two for a long time.* The average sixty-five-year-old man has a life expectancy of eighty-two; for a sixty-five-year-old woman it's eighty-five; and for a married couple the blended probability works out to eighty-nine (a little less than this for two married men, a little more for two married women).† When we "retire" (that is, stop receiving income from our work efforts) we will need income from other sources. Historically, a third of an American's retirement income would come from Social Security, a third from a pension, and a third from assets that they'd saved.

These days, pensions have basically gone by the wayside. If you're a nurse, teacher, or some other sort of local, state, or federal government employee, you probably still have access to one, but for most folks it's unlikely. That means the one-third share that would have come from your pension must also come from your investment assets.

---

*   Jeffrey M. Jones, "More in U.S. Retiring, or Planning to Retire, Later," *Gallup News*, July 22, 2022; Anqi Chen and Alicia H. Munnell, "Pre-Covid Trends in Social Security Claiming," Center for Retirement Research at Boston College, no. 21-9 (May 2021); "2022 Retirement Confidence Survey," report prepared by Employee Benefit Research Institute and Greenwald Research, n.d.

†   Internal Revenue Service, "Distributions from Individual Retirement Arrangements (IRAs)," publication 590-B, April 4, 2023.

I know some people who live on Social Security alone. But in places like the Bay Area, where I live, it is just not possible. There is no way to afford rent or a mortgage and property taxes using nothing but Social Security income. So if you don't have Social Security *and* a pension, you'll be suffering. Likewise, if you don't have investments, you're suffering. How do we reduce suffering? Well, we invest. Investing is the only way to reach all those milestones on the path to financial stability, including a retirement income that we won't outlive. And we're just talking about the basics, the "getting by" folks like my uncle; they too would be better served if they had a little bit more in the way of assets, if they had invested more when they were younger. But they didn't, so they had to work until the age of eighty. For those folks, investing allows them to have more choices — including choosing to work less hard, for less long.

It's a brutal truth that past the age of sixty-five or so, your body starts to give out and you can no longer do the things you did in your forties or fifties. If you don't have investments, what is the other option? It's not a good one.

So you invest.

Responsibility, Part 1: Kids

One thing I always ask my clients at the start of our financial advising relationship is "What is important to you? What is the 'why' behind your investments?" Almost every time, the word *responsibility* comes up. Most couples and parents I have worked with will include responsibility to family as one of their reasons for saving and investing. Once you have a personal sense of security, the idea of securing your family becomes very important. Anyone with kids feels this responsibility keenly.

Warren Buffett says he's not leaving his entire $96 billion fortune to his children; he's planning instead to leave 99 percent to charity. Buffett famously said in a 1986 *Fortune* interview, "I still believe in the philosophy ... that a very rich person should leave his kids enough to do anything but not enough to do nothing."* Buffett's billions are an extreme example of providing for your children, but I love that philosophy. I often struggle with how much to give my own kids, and how that giving (or withholding) will affect their resilience and work ethic. How will the amount of financial support I give my children contribute to the people they become? What lessons do I teach my children and how much should I give — or not — to help instill those lessons? I hate the idea of my kids ever having a feeling of want. Part of that has to do with my upbringing.

The memory of wanting is still in my bones. Since I was raised with little, I still want — and I don't want my kids to grow up with that feeling of insecurity I had. I want them to have the toys and bikes and vacations and experiences I didn't. My wife Kate does incredible work to keep me from going too far with the giving. We have frequent conversations about how we shouldn't spend on ourselves or our kids just because we can. If we give our kids everything they desire, what kind of people will they be in the world? How will they learn the importance of hard work? Will they know how to take directions from a boss? Will they be just like other entitled little rich kids?

My wife grew up with a lot more resources than I did and therefore didn't experience the same type of want. She's

---

*   Richard I. Kirkland Jr. and Carrie Gottlieb, "Should You Leave It All to the Children?," *Fortune*, September 29, 1986.

also done a lot more research on the topic than I have. Her combined expertise and history inform her philosophy that having everything provided for you can ruin your chances of providing for yourself. How can you be resilient if you've never experienced hardship?

It was important to Kate and me that our children have a sense of responsibility and resiliency around finances. So we gave Eli and Annie responsibilities from an early age. As soon as they were able to, the kids had to do their laundry, clean their rooms, and make their own breakfasts, for which we pay them a small allowance. For their allowance, and later their jobs while they're still in school, we made a rule of thirds: a third of their money is theirs to spend, a third goes to savings, and the final third is donated to a charity of their choice.

Once the kids were old enough to work outside the home, they both got jobs at places like the community pool and the local deli. Though their annual incomes started out small — $200 one year, $300 another — we've always claimed the income on their taxes so we could put the money into their own Roth IRAs. Since Eli has been working for a few years now, he's already got a pretty solid Roth IRA going — all income that he earned for himself. He can see it accumulating and he understands how much even a modest retirement account can grow over time.

The great thing is that our kids don't mind working because they know they're working *toward* something, and they get to decide when and how to spend their own money. They know that they can't just go buy anything at the store; they have to *choose* what to buy, and they have to budget for what they want. Sure, Kate and I could technically afford to buy Eli that new game he wanted, or Annie her new bike, but we want our kids to understand that, as the old saying goes, money doesn't grow on trees. Rather, money grows from earning it and investing it.

To be clear, how we spend money on our kids is unique to our own circumstances. Some parents want enough to be able to send their children to college, buy their first car, and help with a down payment on a home. Others want to be able to pay for half of their kids' college or give an initial college farewell payment and then cut the children off. All these preferences are an extremely personal choice and we each must incorporate them into our investment plans.

Responsibility, Part 2: Aging Parents

I had an industry mentor who coached advisers on how to give better financial advice. He said that there is one thing no forty-year-old understands, very few fifty-year-olds understand, maybe a couple of sixty-year-olds understand, but every senior citizen understands: if you're seventy-five years old and you're given the choice (1) to ask your kids for the money on which to live from now on or (2) to die, you will choose to die.

Parents do *not* want to be a burden on their kids. And yet things happen. Maybe your parents couldn't save enough, or maybe they need memory care or other advanced — and prohibitively expensive — treatment. It's important to recognize as early as possible that *you* do not want to be a burden on your children. But wouldn't it be nice to be able to support your parents if they needed it? This, to me, is the other important part of responsibility and a vital reason to invest.

Just as you want to be able to care for your parents or other aging family members should they need it, *you* likely do not want to be a burden on your kids or other family members later in life. If you recognize this as early as possible, and make your investment plan to accommodate this goal, you will save yourself and your family financial misery down the road.

Legendary Legacy

In 1947 Sylvia Bloom took a job as a secretary at Cleary Gottlieb Steen & Hamilton, a Wall Street law firm, where she ended up working for sixty-seven years. Ms. Bloom lived a modest life. She had a rent-controlled apartment, she took the subway, and she made it to work even on the snowiest of days. In 2016, when Ms. Bloom died at the age of ninety-six, she left a staggering $8.2 million to a scholarship fund that helps disadvantaged students go to college.[*]

Her family, friends, and coworkers were shocked. No one had any idea Ms. Bloom had been quietly amassing a fortune. How did she do it? Pretty simple stuff: Over the course of her sixty-seven years at the firm, Ms. Bloom saved what she could and invested her money in amounts that were feasible for her. When she saw what stocks people at work were buying, she'd buy the same ones, just less of them. Over almost seven decades, Ms. Bloom lived simply, amassed millions, and was able to leave a legacy behind. The idea of giving to others was more important to Ms. Bloom than being able to spend on herself. She saved, invested, and gave. In doing so, she was able to affect *many* lives, rather than just her own.

Ms. Bloom is an extreme example, but this idea of a legacy is important. A legacy is what we leave behind when we're gone. If we do the investing thing right, our assets will continue to grow over our entire lives, generating an increasing stream of income to meet our rising cost of living (recall the

---

[*]   Corey Kilgannon, "96-Year-Old Secretary Quietly Amasses Fortune, Then Donates $8.2 Million," *New York Times*, May 6, 2018.

pizza analogy from chapter 3). And at the end of our lives, we will have assets left that can be directed toward our family and/or community's benefit.

Some people tell me they want to make the *perfect* financial plan, which in their eyes is to have just enough money to last their whole lives. They want to spend what they have, and plan it so that they don't leave behind too much, because what good is money when you're dead?

There are a couple of major errors in this way of thinking. First, no one can predict when they will die. Even if doctors were to say that you have only a year to live, what if a new treatment is developed that allows you five more years? Or fifteen? You just *cannot* foresee such a thing. And second, if there were some way to leave money behind to the people and causes you care about, why would you not do that? The beauty of legacy is that any money that outlives us isn't "wasted"; it's allocated toward people and causes that matter to us.

By planning for a retirement income that rises to meet your rising cost of living for some period of time that you cannot predict (what if you live to 110 years old?), you are automatically creating a legacy. Planning to not run out of money in retirement means that something will be left over, right? Put simply, doing the retirement income planning thing right means you will have a legacy to leave behind.

Recall Warren Buffett's $96 billion fortune? Who knows what effects Buffett's billions will have on the world once he's gone, but there's no doubt there will be a ripple effect on the communities he's supporting. You may not have billions or even millions to leave to your favorite charity, but this idea of legacy — no matter the size — is an important one to keep in mind. And unless you're one of the lucky few, the only way to get you there is by investing.

Shifting from "How Will I Survive?" to "How Can I Be Significant?"

When I turned forty, I revisited my financial plan, as I do every year. But for that big birthday, I did a deep dive on my goals. I saw that at about age forty-five I'd be making enough money, my investments would be in good-enough places, that we'd be okay.

Realizing that we were in that place of security, I thought about what was important to me. I've already got my plan in place so that I can have the things I need to make me happy. What can I do for others? Again, this will be different for everyone. Maybe you want to contribute to a scholarship fund that helped pay for your college; maybe you want to start your own scholarship fund or support community-building efforts.

The "Big Why" with investing starts with the question of how you can take care of your family and yourself for a lifetime, recognizing that for a third of that period you almost certainly won't be working (either by choice or perhaps your mind or body won't let you do it anymore). Then, once you have that why, you move up the pyramid and are able to do something significant for a community you care about.

At the Heart of It Is Love

The idea of investing is often associated with greed. We think of those Wall Street guys (recall *The Wolf of Wall Street* scene we talked about in chapter 2), and we might feel guilt by association. In the next chapter, we'll explore some of the biases we have about investing that can hinder smart and stable financial choices. But for now, let's dispel one myth around investing: that greed must have anything to do with it. To me, all the reasons we should invest — security, responsibility, legacy — are wrapped up in a word that's far from greed: love.

At the heart of every reason for investing is love. Even lifestyle is part of this calculation: we look at what we love in this world, what makes us happy, and we build a financial plan around that lifestyle that takes into account the people we love too.

For those of us with kids, planning, saving, and investing for their education is a function of our wanting the best for them. We do this out of love. The same goes for the reasons behind caring for aging or ailing family members. Maybe your parents didn't plan well, maybe they were unlucky, or maybe one of them got sick and was forced to spend more than they ever expected. Having the resources available to support our family members when they're unable to support themselves is something we do out of love. We don't want to see those we love suffer; if we have the capacity, we want to help them.

With deep and regular practice of Buddhist *metta*, or loving-kindness meditation, the idea of the "family" you want to keep from suffering expands. It might include a neighbor, a member of your church, or someone identified through a local charity — whenever a fellow human suffers, we want to help. This is the opposite of greed. This is love.

Legacy isn't necessarily something that needs to wait until we've left this earth either. We can support efforts that align with our values and give as we are able. By the time I was forty-eight, my income had increased enough that I was making more than my family and I needed to fund our long-term plans. With this realization, my wife and I decided to start giving more. We set up a scholarship fund to help kids attend college, assisted the local homeless shelter in building a new facility, and supported a local health clinic for undocumented people in our community. I know what it's like to feel insecure. Now that I'm in a better place in my life, it's important to me to be able to help others get on their feet too.

Legacy is something we do out of love for our family and our community. Some people leave assets behind to give their kids a head start. Some people leave money for their extended family or their community to support organizations and nonprofits that were important to them in life. This too is love.

At the core of both of my books — *Mindful Money* and *Mindful Investing* — is mindfulness. As we're defining it here, mindfulness is the nonjudgmental awareness of reality as it presents itself. As I've said over and over in these pages, one day we will all need a source of income that we can rely on when our working income won't cut it. This is a reality. For most of us, we will need this source of income for twenty-plus years in a rising-cost world — and we should plan on thirty-plus. Investing for retirement income is also a show of love, because if we don't have those funds we will have to rely on the limited resources of our kids or our communities.

This kind of basic reliance on others will likely *not* be the type of great retirement most people hope to have. Fortunately, we *can* plan and invest enough so that we get to enjoy the dignity of self-reliance in our retirement. As my coach said, many of us would rather die than be a burden on our kids (or our communities). Recognizing this early and investing for our own retirement is a form of loving those around us.

The Constraints of Time

For each of these investing goals, time is of the essence. There may be a little variation in when we retire and when we may be called on to support our parents, and there is certainly variation in when we die (and can leave a legacy) — but the differences aren't large. We know when kids need to go to school. And if we talk to our parents, we will learn when they might run out of money and need help (though they may never admit it). One of the reasons we plan is so that we can line up these needs and desires in order of priority and make sure we are saving enough and investing in the right way to make them all come together in the time we have, creating income streams that are available when we need them.

Next, we're going to look at the psychology of investing, and how our biases creep in and inform the investment decisions we do or don't make.

MINDFUL INVESTING ACTIVITY

It's time to do some simple math. In your notebook, figure out how many working years you are likely to have until retirement. The average age of retirement in the United States is sixty-two; unless you have a highly atypical career or lifestyle, you should do your initial planning based on that number. So sixty-two minus your current age is the number of years you have to accumulate the money you'll need for retirement. If you're already sixty-two or older, or if you took an early retirement, lucky you! In that case, your math problem is to subtract your current age from one hundred. That's how long you should plan to stretch your retirement assets — which hopefully you're still accumulating.

In each of these cases — pre- and postretirement — you should keep the number in your head and use it to evaluate the wisdom of any long- or short-term financial decisions. There are many helpful tools for figuring out whether you'll have enough for retirement and, if not, how you can catch up — including my first book, *Mindful Money*, which has step-by-step instructions for doing just this.

CHAPTER 5

The Psychology of Investing

Let Wall Street have a nightmare and the whole country
has to help them get back into bed again.
— WILL ROGERS

In the late 2000s, I had a potential client I'll call Andy. In our first meeting, Andy sat down and told me he needed help. I said, "Okay, tell me your story." Andy shared that in the late '90s he was killing it, making all kinds of money, and really excited about it. He told his advisers, "This is great! Let's go big, let's make *more* money!"

Then the year 2000 hit and Andy lost big in the dot-com crash — something like 50 to 60 percent of his investments. Furious, he fired all his advisers. He didn't think he could afford any more losses, so he instructed his new advisers to be *very* careful. Andy's new team told him how to invest to not lose more money in the stock market, protecting his financial future as requested. They put Andy's money in low-volatility/low-risk and fixed income investments like bonds, CDs, and other defensive choices. And then, when the market took off, Andy's portfolio didn't recover. He got all upset once more, fired *those* advisers, and started looking for someone who could, at the least, keep up with the markets.

By 2005 or 2006 Andy had hired another adviser and told them he *really* wanted to be in a position to grow his money. He said that when the markets recovered previously, he didn't really make any money (this, of course, was because his assets were in fixed income accounts, which are lower-return long term but don't fluctuate with the market ups and downs like stocks do). Andy was upset that his portfolio hadn't recovered when the markets recovered and was determined to, once again, invest in a way that could substantially grow his wealth.

His new adviser invested Andy's money back into equities and real estate. These are choices that may benefit from greater long-term returns, but also have a lot more volatility attached to them. More volatility means a higher chance of bigger payoffs and, of course, of bigger losses. And indeed, when the housing crash of 2007–8 happened, the markets tanked, and Andy lost a whole bunch of money. He got really upset and fired yet another adviser.

You can see the pattern here. I can see the pattern here. Andy couldn't see the pattern.

The moral of the story is that it's not the adviser, it's the individual's inability to know what they really want and to stay the course. Andy couldn't do either, and it hurt him time and again. He had to switch and switch and switch, trying to find an adviser whose market outlook about the future inspired his trust.

This is one of the most consistent investing mistakes people make — looking to what worked in past market circumstances and assuming it will continue to work in the future. This always eventually fails. There is *no* evidence for the persistence of performance, hence the small print in so many ads stating that "past performance is no guarantee of future success." It really, really isn't. The key to smart investing is committing to a process. You have to make a long-term commitment to some amount of risk (the percentage of your portfolio in equities), and it is your commitment (along with regular rebalancing to that commitment) that gets you there.

Every time Andy went into a new adviser's office, he brought along all his unexamined biases about how the market works. That always backfires. So before we get into discussion of how to make the right investments for our needs, it's crucial to understand the biases we all have and the limitations of our knowledge. Once we understand how those biases and limitations play out, it'll be much easier to leave them at the door when making an investment plan.

Philosophy and the Limitations of Knowledge

Andy made two dangerous mistakes regarding his financial decisions. The first was that he had neither a philosophy nor a process to serve as the basis for an investment plan. In any of the scenarios described above, if Andy had had a market philosophy, a simple portfolio management process, and an investment plan he stuck with, he would have been far better off.

The idea is to *stick with the plan*. Markets zig and zag regularly, but then they recover. The zig sows the seeds of the zag; the zag sows the seeds of the zig. Look back at my brief history of investing in chapter 2 if you need a reminder. After the Great Depression, the dot-com crash, and the Covid-19-related dips, the markets recovered every time. It's important to zoom out and look at the big picture. In figure 2 (see next page) you can see all the peaks and valleys over the last hundred-plus years.

But what you can also see is that the overall trend is positive. The longer we hold our portfolios (regardless of which portfolio design method we choose, except for short-term trading), the higher the probability that they go up.

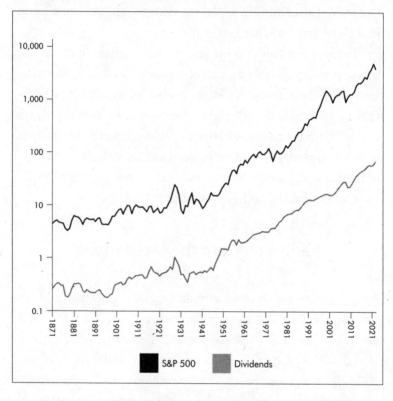

Figure 2. US equity markets 1871–2022. Human innovation and productivity overcome fear. Markets zig and zag but trend up: stick with the plan.*

---

* Data from 1871–1927 are from Dr. Robert Shiller's (Yale) historical market data archive, http://www.econ.yale.edu/~shiller/data.htm. Data from 1928–2022 are from Dr. Aswath Damodaran of the NYU Stern School of Business, https://pages.stern.nyu.edu/~adamodar/New_Home_Page /home.htm. Pre-1928 data represent most of the companies then trading on the New York Stock Exchange (still in its infancy); 1928–1956 data represent the S&P 90; 1957–2022 data represent the S&P 500.

Your philosophy needs to incorporate the understanding that markets collapse and recover all the time. We *must* accept the limitations of our knowledge; we *cannot* predict the short-term future, so why do we keep trying? When the markets are down, we may be losing money, or *fear* losing money, and decide to sell our current portfolio to "protect" ourselves from this possibility, which does not work any better. There is no escaping these six fundamental investing truths:

1. We will experience both greed and fear when we invest.
2. Markets are inherently unpredictable.
3. This unpredictability doesn't stop anyone from trying to predict them.
4. Some of those who try will get it right and scream it from rooftops.
5. No one can know in advance which predictions will be right. Those who do get it right are *lucky*, not skillful. (Remember that *Wolf of Wall Street* scene? It's all fugazi.)
6. Most important of all: *you don't need to get it right to be successful.*

A nonjudgmental awareness of our limitations allows us to separate our diversified portfolio's relative short-term performance from our fear that we are doing something wrong. The siren song of outperformance is always attractive, until we crash on the rocks.

What We Don't Know and Can't Know

According to a 2016 CNN/ORC poll, the majority of Americans believed that the United States was still in a recession in early 2016, despite the fact that we'd been out of the last recession for over half a decade.* For the first time in our history, a 2013 Pew Research Center survey found that most Americans were convinced their children will be worse off than they have been at similar points in their lives.† We tend to believe that markets and the economies surrounding them are fragile, unstable, and vulnerable. We have no sense of history, so we think that current negative economic, political, and market events are likely to bring about our financial demise.

We often make financial decisions based on what's going on right now — or what we *perceive* to be going on — in the economy. For example, you see that the markets are down so you decide to liquidate your portfolios because you're afraid they will go down further. That decision is driven by bias and fear as much as by any intelligent strategy.

The same thing happens on the upside. When markets are going up, up, up, many people drastically reduce their diversification in order to put it all in the thing that's hot at the moment. Bitcoin is a notable example of this. When the cryptocurrency came out in 2009, some people knew about it but no one was really paying attention. A few made some big money and that made some headlines. The price of Bitcoin went up, more people got interested, and it became this self-fulfilling cycle until it eventually imploded.

Of course, I have no idea where Bitcoin is going, and this is *not* a prediction.‡ Still, the idea that the driving force behind Bitcoin's success is the attention that we pay it, *not* the

---

*   Heather Long, "56% of Americans Think Their Kids Will Be Worse Off," CNN.com, January 28, 2016.

†   "Economies of Emerging Markets Better Rated during Difficult Times: Global Downturn Takes Heavy Toll; Inequality Seen as Rising," report conducted by the Pew Research Center, May 23, 2013.

‡   I repeat: this is *not* a prediction.

additional value it's providing, is an interesting conundrum. That's our limitation of knowledge at work. We tend to believe what we read and see online, and that the amount of buzz around a thing correlates with its quality, but it doesn't. It's just that more people are talking about the same thing. This has happened throughout history, from the Dutch tulip bubble in the 1600s, to the South Sea bubble of 1720, to Japan's stock bubble (which burst in 1991), and many others we've discussed already. Each time, the buzz far outweighed the reality.

We tend to look for things that will confirm what we already believe. The news we read and the social media accounts we follow tend to back up or echo our own belief systems, and we do the exact same thing with investing. All too often, we begin investing with biases we don't even know we have.

Release the Biases!

One of the most important things you can do for your financial success is to make an unwavering investing plan with a long-term outlook in mind. Unfortunately, our biases creep in and try to thwart this long-term mindset. Resist!

Our biases — and we all have them — work to enforce a focus on the short term, which is how our brains are hardwired. We evolved on the African savanna, and our neurochemistry often reacts as if we still might meet a lion coming out of the bushes. When we experience market decline, our biases and our amygdala (the gland responsible for releasing cortisol and adrenaline, our "fight or flight" hormones) are stimulated to act. And our actions are directly opposed to our long-term financial success.

So how do we help control these biases from taking over our investment decisions? The first step is understanding.

Bias Blindness

George Bernard Shaw famously said, "Progress is impossible without change; and those who cannot change their minds cannot change anything."* This same concept can be applied to investing. We all have unperceived biases informing how we make decisions. "Bias blindness" is the idea that we have a difficult time seeing our own preconceptions. As we explore each of these, it might be worth asking yourself if and how these biases have shown up in your own investment thinking.

Confirmation Bias

After the 2020 election, about a third of the country believed the election was stolen. This theory has been tested by rank-and-file Republicans, GOP-driven court systems, and GOP governors — and the idea of a "stolen election" was disproved over and over. And yet, as I write this book two years later, pretty much the same proportion of Americans still believes it to be true. How is it that we can have facts, and yet we still disagree on what the facts *are*? This is the work of bias at its finest: We think we are sorting through data and making rational choices, but *really* what we're doing is looking for data that validates what we already believe. Once we find data that supports our opinions, we put it in the yes column and treat it as trustworthy and valuable.

This is confirmation bias, the error by which we overvalue any data points that confirm what we already believe and discard any that contradict it. If the headline disagrees with what we believe, we're going to put that idea on the back burner and we *might* get back to it later, after we've looked at all the stuff

---

* George Bernard Shaw, *Everybody's Political What's What?* (London: Constable, 1944), 330.

we already know and agree with. We are constantly looking for evidence to back up what we already believe.

An example of how this plays out in investing? Tesla.

For years we've been told that Tesla is *the* electric car to buy and to invest in, that it's changing the vehicle world. Tesla is the leading EV on the market, and the company has an enormous valuation that is far above its earnings — making Elon Musk (as I write this) the wealthiest person on the face of the earth. It makes no sense at all! So why is Tesla stock valued so high? Because of all the people drinking the Tesla Kool-Aid. They're just *believing* in Tesla, feeding off one another's belief, and jointly pushing the price up.

This is all confirmation bias at work. We find a company that's sensationalized on a subreddit, we talk among ourselves, and we pick the company that we're *hearing* most about, not caring so much what that company sells, what it does, or whether it's even profitable. We're all just going to pile on and inflate the price. And if we do that, does that mean there's more value? No.

Value is based on revenues, profitability, and dividends. Price is what you pay for a share of those items of value. Alas, price can get dislocated from value because of the subreddit and meme stocks, and it's almost always confirmation bias that drives things in that direction. (We will explore other examples of meme stocks in chapter 15.)

I'd much prefer to own stock in Ford as it transitions into an EV company, because the price is low and as it pivots its sizable resources and experience it might crush Tesla.* Of course, I have no idea whether that'll happen — maybe Tesla will end up using its equity to buy Ford, Mercedes, or something like that. Regardless, no matter what the company

---

* This is not a recommendation.

does, Tesla's valuation — its price as compared to its earnings, book value, and cash flow — will eventually rightsize. Either the stock price will have to come down, or the company's revenues, profits, and dividends will have to go up (which will be harder as more entrenched competitors start to enter the EV market). Just because a stock has gone up in price doesn't mean it's going to continue doing so. And just because everyone is saying it's a good buy doesn't mean that it is.

Herding: Going with What Everyone Else Is Doing

If you think of the term *herd mentality*, you probably picture a flock of sheep moving blindly in the same direction. The idea is that we tend to do the things the people around us are doing. Our collective fear and excitement are fueled by the media in general and by social media in particular.

With investing, an excellent example of herding is the meme-stock phenomenon. This happens when a stock becomes popular on social media because everyone is talking about it, whether that's GameStop, National Beverage, or this month's new hotness. Then (typically young and inexperienced) investors start buying shares of that stock. More people talk about it and more people buy it, driving the price up and up until that stock isn't hot anymore. The company itself may not be rising in value at all, but because of the perceived value — the rising price of that hot stock — people think they're in on a special deal.

Sure, some people who are closely watching can make a lot of money playing the meme-stock game. But most people lose — especially if you're talking long-term. I find it much easier and safer to avoid the hype and stick with my plan.

Recency Bias:
What Just Happened Is What We Believe

If you were a small child when the World Trade Center came down, you might have watched the coverage on the news, which showed the towers falling on a loop. You didn't necessarily recognize that those were the same buildings in different footage. It happened on CNN, it happened on CNBC, it happened on NBC, it happened on ABC. Every channel was showing this footage 24/7 for weeks.

At that age, your brain didn't differentiate between which tower was which, and you saw the coverage so much that you may well have gotten to the point of wondering how many more buildings were going to fall. A child might not have realized that it was the same media story, told over and over again.

When markets fall, it's the same media story and it's told a thousand times, from every angle. This type of bombardment affects our brains and how we make decisions. It's what we see right now that affects our reactions in the moment.

The stuff that's most vivid is what we've seen most recently, and that recently seen data drives our behaviors in a way that the knowledge of the last market's decline or recovery does not. It is much harder to remember a market recovery that happened a decade ago than it is to remember the worry-inducing headlines of today.

Recency bias causes us to assume that wherever our portfolios were last month is where they'll keep going. I call this straight-line thinking: the belief that things that have happened recently are likely to continue (if XYZ investment has done well, it will keep doing well).

More of My Favorite Biases

The goal with investing is to focus on the long-term plan, which as we've seen is not always easy or intuitive. Below is a summary of some further biases that work to enforce a focus on the short term, thus inhibiting our investment decisions.

- **Overconfidence:** Everyone can be prone to overconfidence, but it's particularly important for men to acknowledge how it might affect our investment decisions.*
- **Familiarity bias:** We are more likely to invest in things that feel familiar to us. US investors buy US stocks; San Francisco investors like tech stocks; New York investors like banking and financial stocks; and so forth.
- **Anchoring bias:** This describes the tendency to mentally "anchor" on a preconceived price. Let's say you have a stock that's worth ten dollars. If it goes up to twenty dollars and then drops to fifteen, you might not want to sell until it gets back to twenty, even if selling now would still turn a profit. You're "anchored" on twenty dollars.
- **Mental accounting:** We treat our original principal and our gains differently. People don't like to risk their original principal but have less of a problem with the idea of losing their gains.

---

* Brad M. Barber and Terrance Odean, "Boys Will Be Boys: Gender, Overconfidence, and Common Stock Investment," *Quarterly Journal of Economics* 116, no. 1 (2001): 261–92; Gerlinde Fellner-Röhling and Sebastian Krügel, "Judgmental Overconfidence and Trading Activity," *Journal of Economic Behavior and Organization* 107, pt. B (November 2014): 827–42; Sabine Hügelschäfer and Anja Achtziger, "On Confident Men and Rational Women: It's All on Your Mind(set)," *Journal of Economic Psychology* 41 (April 2014): 31–44.

- **Selective memory:** People tend to remember their wins (or the wins they hear about) and forget their losses over time. This gives them a better picture of their brilliance than they deserve. This is why I love hearing investors feel comfortable enough to talk about their losses, and I always take their win stories with a grain of salt.

Even More Challenges to Being a Human Investor

In chapter 3, I talked about three key challenges to being a human investor: the aforementioned biases, our general lack of financial education, and the overload of information out there. There is another issue we face with investing that I call the three *P*'s: physiology, psychology, and pro-cyclical thinking.

We've touched briefly on the physiology piece already. That is, our brains are wired to jump and run at perceived threats, and our neurochemistry isn't nuanced enough to know the difference between a lion about to pounce and headlines predicting imminent economic collapse. We feel the fear and react — and often that reaction goes against our plan (if we've even made one). Andy is a great example of what happens when physiology takes over.

The second *P* is psychology, which refers to the cognitive and emotional biases we just explored. This is best identified by Amos Tversky and Daniel Kahneman's Nobel Prize–winning prospect theory, the idea that investors respond differently to losses than we do to gains.[*] Also known as loss aversion, this

---

[*]   James Chen, "Prospect Theory: What It Is and How It Works, with Examples," Investopedia.com, updated July 22, 2022; Daniel Kahneman and Amos Tversky, "Prospect Theory: An Analysis of Decision under Risk," *Econometrica* 47, no. 2 (1979): 263–92.

theory says that losing money feels twice as bad as making the same amount of money feels good. Say someone gives you $5,000; that feels good, right? But then if you lose that same $5,000, it feels significantly worse than the gain felt good.

An even simpler example: Say a person puts a dollar into a slot machine. They pull the lever and they win a hundred-dollar jackpot! They print out the winning ticket and are in a good, smiley mood. Later that night, that person loses their hundred-dollar ticket and they are *crushed*. They spend an hour looking for it, never find it, and their whole night is ruined. Win one hundred dollars, feeling pleasant. Lose one hundred dollars, feeling devastated. The moral is that we tend to place a much greater value on avoiding a loss than we do on making a gain.

The third *P* is pro-cyclical thinking, meaning that we tend to process markets pro-cyclically instead of counter-cyclically. An example of this? Soup. Say you like Campbell's Condensed Chicken Noodle Soup and it's usually two dollars a can. One day, you go to the store and it's twenty-five cents a can. Exciting! You stock up on soup while it's cheap — that makes sense. That is an example of counter-cyclical thinking in action: prices go down and because you get more for your money, the value goes up. That is a good thing, right? Unfortunately, this is not how we process markets.

In markets, when prices go down, people believe the value is falling. If a share of Apple stock rises from $140 to $150, that's seen as a good thing because the price is going up. But if the price fell to, say, $85, we would hear about the decline as a horrible thing. We might say, "What's wrong at Apple? The stock is down 30 percent!" It would still be the same company, still make great products, still create tons of value, and now the stock would be cheaper to buy. Why wouldn't you be just as excited about the reduced Apple stock as you were about cheap chicken noodle soup? And how should we *actually* expect our investments to behave? We'll explore these concepts in the next chapter.

MINDFUL INVESTING ACTIVITY

The number one way to avoid making mistakes based on your biases is to develop self-awareness, in conjunction with making sure you're getting good information. Take a moment to think back over decisions you've made that, in the light of this chapter, you realize might have been based more on bias than any sensible strategy. If you don't have a lot of experience with investing, you may not have a lot of market-based examples to draw on, but bias is bias.

For example, there are all kinds of ways overconfidence can get us in trouble, not just in investing. Have you ever found yourself unprepared and out of your depth due to overconfidence? Whether it's investing in a stock you "just know" is going to be great or deciding to try a double-black-diamond ski run the day you master the bunny slope, your overconfidence did not serve you well.

In your notebook, write down a few examples of times you made a decision or went along with a plan without enough information and had a negative outcome. For this thought exercise, that outcome could be anything from public embarrassment to missed opportunities to financial setbacks.

Now, looking over the list below, can you identify

biases that led to these unfavorable outcomes? Note them alongside the examples in your notebook. Do any patterns emerge?

- Confirmation bias
- Herding
- Recency bias
- Overconfidence
- Familiarity bias
- Anchoring bias
- Mental accounting
- Selective memory

PART 2

How to Invest

CHAPTER 6

Before You Invest

We are all, it seems, saving ourselves for the senior prom.
But many of us forget that somewhere
along the way we must learn to dance.

— ALAN HARRINGTON

I have clients come to me with plans to buy a house by the age of thirty-five, retire by sixty, and support their kids through college — all noble and achievable goals. For some clients, we get started right away: we pull from savings and set up Roth IRAs (a retirement fund that allows for investing and is not taxed upon disbursement); buy diversified funds with recurring, regular contributions; and then play the waiting game (with regular rebalancing)* for thirty-plus years. Some clients, however, come to me and are not *ready* to invest. While we still want to get started as soon as possible, some prep work may be needed. If your finances aren't set up correctly, you

---

* Rebalancing means you're periodically realigning the weightings of your portfolio by buying or selling certain assets to keep your original, planned asset allocation. Not sure what that means? No problem, we'll go into lots of detail on rebalancing in chapter 12. For now, think "buy low, sell high."

may end up having to pull from your investment accounts and wind up back where you started.

The whole idea with investing, as we've discussed, is the long-term outlook, which includes patience, discipline, and planning — including a plan for the unplannable.

Emergency Fund for the Inevitable Emergencies

As the saying goes, "shit happens." No one can predict an accident, an unexpected medical diagnosis, or a severe storm. Cars break down, trees fall on houses, layoffs happen. Expenses like these can cost thousands of dollars; if we don't have a pocket of money we can reach into, such emergencies can cause enormous setbacks.

In chapter 22 of *Mindful Money* we go into more detail about how to build an emergency fund, but the high-level idea is this: Save cash for when you need it. And when you least expect it, you *will* need it. The last thing you want to do is to set up your investments, watch them grow for a few years, then have to pull from those accounts at a bad time and set back all the progress you've made.

But how much cash should you have on hand? The older we get, the more cushion we need. Early in adulthood, we don't have as many expenses, we tend to have fewer financial responsibilities and dependents, and our life risk is lower. Then life grows more complex. Again, this is a high-level overview, but here are some guidelines for savings depending on our age:

- Young adults (eighteen to thirty-five): three months of living expenses.
- Middle years (thirty-six to fifty-five): six to twelve months of living expenses.

- Nearing retirement (fifty-six until retirement): twelve to twenty-four months of living expenses.
- In retirement: two years of living expenses.

Emergencies take many forms. One painfully recent example is the Covid-19 pandemic. Nearly ten million Americans lost their jobs, and for many that job loss dramatically affected their financial situation. People had to live off savings or obliterate their 401Ks (if they had them), and many still struggled to pay their rent or mortgage. Some of my clients or their partners lost their jobs during the pandemic, which created a huge strain. But the clients who had ample savings accounts were able to refrain from pulling money from their investments because they had saved up enough cash to serve as a buffer while they were unemployed or earned drastically reduced incomes.

There are less monumental emergencies, of course. Things like high but non-catastrophic medical bills, those inevitable car repairs, or needing to replace appliances. A few years ago, my wife and I had to buy a new refrigerator. That fridge worked great until right after the warranty was over, at which point it started ruining food. The freezer would thaw our frozen items and the fridge would freeze our produce. Lots of rotten vegetables, four different repair people, and thousands of dollars later, one technician finally discovered and repaired the ventilation problem that was causing the mess, but phew! that fridge turned out to be an expensive appliance. You just never know.

For these types of emergencies, you want to have enough of a buffer saved up that you can pull from your cash account, repair your fridge, and move on with your life. But even those folks who *have* savings accounts often feel compelled to use their credit cards for these types of expenses because they like the idea of keeping that savings account balance. If you *have* your emergency fund, use it for what it's for — emergencies! Avoid using credit cards unless you're able to pay them off each month, and particularly avoid using them once they're paid off.

If you *can* pay off your credit balances each month, regular use of credit cards helps increase your credit score and maintain your good standing with credit card companies. This is also a great way to utilize rewards like cash back or travel redemptions.

Speaking of credit, paying off high-interest credit and other debts is the second step you should take *before* you start investing.

Paying Off Debts and Eliminating Bad Interest

First, why does paying off debts matter? Part of it is psychological. Having debt is a major stressor. There is a feeling of freedom and control that comes from *not* having debt and knowing that your money is going toward something for your future — not back toward something that already happened.

Having debts can also negatively affect your credit score, which leads to higher interest rates on loans you may need in the future (for big expenses such as education, mortgages, and cars) or even the inability to borrow at all until you get those debts paid off and your credit score raised.

Maybe you're thinking, "But I want to get started investing in my retirement as soon as I can!" That is wise. However, part of the equation here is some simple math: we lose far more money paying 10 percent, 15 percent, 20 percent, or even 29 percent compound interest charges on credit cards and loans than we can ever reasonably expect to earn by investing. Why start paying, say, $100 a month into an investment account that earns 7 percent returns when your credit card is charging you 22 percent interest, compounding on itself monthly? You'd be *losing* financial ground by investing that $100 a month right now instead of using it to pay down your debt.

Every penny of your income that goes toward your debts is income that is *not* going to your savings and investment accounts. If you have debts, you want to start eliminating them as soon as possible. So how aggressively should you chip away at those bills? A common pitfall to avoid is attacking your debt so aggressively that you sacrifice your emergency cash reserves. Then you will be in double trouble if a crisis strikes. That's why paying off debt comes *after* you create an emergency fund.

We go into this in more detail in chapter 23 of *Mindful Money*, but a good rule of thumb is that as soon as you have your emergency fund in place, stop contributing to it and start paying that same amount of money each month toward your debts. Do not start spending that money! Think of that monthly amount as a bill that you *must* pay until you reach your goals.

Where to begin? First, pay off your highest interest debts. Say you have two credit cards: one with 29 percent interest, one with 12.99 percent interest. You'd want to make minimum payments on that 12.99 percent account while putting all the extra cash you have toward that 29 percent account. Once that high-interest card is paid off, all the money that you were putting into paying down that card should now go toward that 12.99 percent card until it is fully paid off.

Some of my clients can pay off their credit cards extraordinarily quickly using this method. They simply hadn't had a plan in place and hadn't looked at where their accounts were before they started investing. If there's one thing to remember here, it's that compounding interest can be an incredible enemy when it comes to debt — but an exceptional friend when it comes to investing.

Make Way for the Eighth Wonder of the World: Compound Interest

You've probably heard the phrase "Let your money work for *you*." One of the smartest ways to do that is by utilizing the power of compound interest, which is when you earn interest on both the initial principal sum and on the interest that sum has made. Simply put, making interest on interest.

When I was a kid, I had what they called a passbook savings account at the Black Hills Federal Credit Union. Each time I made a deposit — two dollars here, five dollars there — the teller would put a stamp in my book, show me my balance, and show how much interest I'd earned. I can't recall now how much the account started with, but for simplicity's sake let's say it was fifty dollars. At 5 percent interest, without adding to the account at all, after one month that account would have earned twenty-one cents, for a balance of $50.21 ($50 × [0.05/12] = $0.21). In the ninth month, it would earn twenty-two cents per month; by the end of the second year, it would be earning twenty-three cents per month; and so on. The percentage of return stays the same, but the amount of interest grows because you're earning interest on interest. It was a small amount, but as a kid it was exciting to watch the teller scribble down the interest my money had earned and add it to my balance. Something about having that tangible reminder that I was earning more and more money was incredibly motivating.

The chart below shows what would have happened to that account I opened in 1980 if I'd added nothing to it and just allowed compound interest to do its magic. To make it a little more interesting, the two columns on the right are based on my having instead deposited $5,000 into that same account. Of course, if I were also adding to the account each month, I'd be in even better shape, but the bottom line is to demonstrate the simple gift of compound interest. It's exciting to see what can happen, even when you start with something as small as fifty dollars. You have to start somewhere, right?

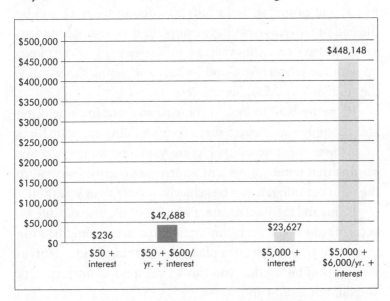

Figure 3. Compound interest terminal value, 1980–2022[*]

Compound interest can work against you as well, as in the case of many student loans these days. Let's look at the example of someone who got a $40,000 loan with a compounding

[*] Source: "Historical Returns on Stocks, Bonds and Bills: 1928–2022," NYU Stern School of Business, January 2023.

interest rate of 5.9 percent. After the first year, if they haven't made a payment, that original $40,000 debt has "grown" to $42,360. Or, if they paid "interest only" for the first year, that $2,360 in interest would be paid, but they'd still owe the original $40,000. If, as I hope is the case for anyone with student loans, you are paying the current interest *and* a portion of the principal over a twenty-year payment plan, then by the end of the second year you would have paid $6,822.48 (which means only $2,226 off the principal and over $4,500 in interest); by the tenth year you would have paid $34,112 (but only $14,279 in principal, and nearly $20,000 in interest); and by the end of a twenty-year payment plan, that $40,000 student loan will have cost you $28,225 in interest. If you can't keep up with the payments? Good luck. It's no wonder they call it the student loan crisis. See figure 4.

It's pretty hard to look at those figures, but imagine being able to apply the interest that's compounding on your loans to an investment account. Picture your investment account earning that same 5.9 percent return over twenty years. With the right planning, it can be achieved sooner than you think.

Loans and credit cards are, for many of us, unavoidable aspects of adulthood. Still, eliminating that debt should be a top priority in your investment planning. Get rid of those debts as soon as possible so that you can let compound interest work *for* you, not *against* you.

Investment Education: Now and Always

In my early forties I started taking my health more seriously. I began replacing (most) pizza nights with healthier alternatives. Lots of fish, chicken, and vegetables. I began exercising regularly and got in pretty good shape. I lost thirty pounds. I felt great! But during the times when I've loosened up on

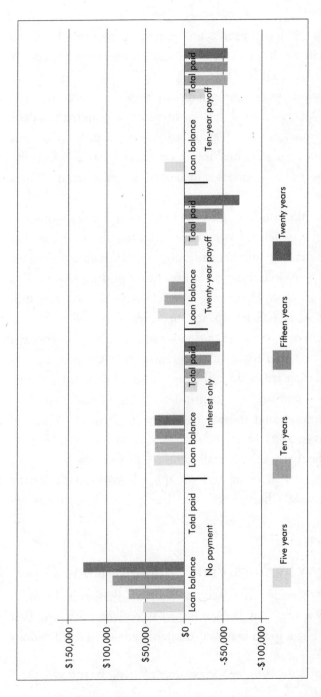

Figure 4. Amortization of loan of $40,000 over twenty years with four monthly payment approaches: no payment ($0); interest only ($197); twenty-year payoff ($284); ten-year payoff ($442)

my routine, stopped exercising, started eating out a little too much, that weight just creeps back up on me. I have to stay at it regularly to keep in shape.

The same kind of thing happens with our investment education. We can learn about our finances, we can make a debt reduction plan, a savings plan, and an investment plan, but if we're not regularly checking in on those plans and learning new things to keep ourselves in shape it's easy to fall back into old habits.

It is vital to understand how market economies work and to continue to refresh your knowledge on the topic so that when the markets fluctuate and our portfolios are affected we know what to do (which is almost always nothing).

Keep in mind that markets will always zig and zag, bull and bear. They will go up, up, up, then they will go down, down, then maybe up, then down even further. It's two steps forward, one step back, but remember that the overall, big-picture market trend since the beginning of time is that markets will — eventually — continue going up. Recall that chart from chapter 5 that showed the US stock market's historical returns from 1871 to the present? Yes, there are dips, but you can see clearly that the overall trend is up. Take any thirty-year snippet from that chart and you'll see how dramatically the market grows. That growth can be in your investment accounts.

Your Why, Your Plan, and Your Trade-Offs

In his 1758 essay "The Way to Wealth," Benjamin Franklin famously wrote, "An investment in knowledge pays the best interest."* The piece is full of quotable advice around money

---

*   Quoted in the *Daily Evening Transcript* (Boston), February 16, 1849.

and the psychology of money. It is a great demonstration of how we must consistently and regularly check in on the habits we have worked so hard to create. Below I share two excerpts I want to explore. Here's the first:

> You may think, perhaps, that a little tea, or a little punch now and then, a diet a little more costly, clothes a little finer, and a little entertainment now and then, can be no great matter; but remember, "Many a little makes a mickle."* Beware of little expenses; a small leak will sink a great ship.

Here's another. Keep in mind, this was written in 1758:

> We knew in a neighboring city, four blacksmiths employed in the same shop — two were first-rate workmen, the other two were helpers. The first two received $1.50 per day each; the last two 75 cents per day. The first two were regular drinkers, and no persuasion could induce them to forego their drams; the last two were temperate men and extended nothing for strong drink. Now mark the difference. The first two were poor — their families neglected, destitute, and distressed. The wife and children of one of them have been driven from their beds into the street, in a cold night, and compelled to accept of charity to save them from starvation. At length, he deserted his family, and soon after died suddenly at Pittsburgh. The other is now very sick, apparently on his deathbed. The two helpers who received about 75 cents per day, support their families comfortably, and have each about $300 in the Savings' Bank.

---

* A *mickle* is a large amount.

Sure, this anecdote depicts two fellows who were alcoholics, the obvious reason for their overspending and the demise of their families. But the sentiment rings true and is something I've seen many times in my career: a person making $150,000 a year can have *less* savings, *more* debt, and worse credit than a person who makes $75,000 a year. How? Planning (or the lack thereof).

Once you've determined your goals, you must next determine how much you'll need to commit to saving, and how much those savings need to grow over your lifetime. Once you've determined how much you need to commit to saving each month, each year you'll have to determine what percentage of return you'll need from your portfolio to meet those goals.

Say you've determined what returns you'll need to see to reach your savings goals, and you realize that you'll need more returns on your portfolio than the market or your risk tolerance can support. If that's the case, it's time to reassess either your goals or what you're willing to give up to make those goals happen, whether that means working a little longer than you'd hoped, increasing your risk (more on that later), or giving up certain things you're used to having in order to save more.

The first step I take with any client in making their investment plan is to help determine their Big Whys. I ask, "What is important to you, both the big picture and the small?" This is largely what *Mindful Money* is about, so we won't go into depth on that here, but we cannot dig deeper into making an investment plan without this mindset: you will have to make trade-offs.

For many people, these trade-offs add up to a lot.*

---

* Budgeting is a huge part of making this plan, which we cover in the third section of *Mindful Money*. As a first step I highly recommend looking at your assets and liabilities and seeing where your money is really going each month.

Some people *love* going out to eat. Great! If that's your thing, budget for at least one great meal out every month. Some people don't care so much about the dining experience but love a good glass of wine. Then eat at home and splurge on your favorite bottles from the Loire Valley. Maybe you care less about cars, so you continue to maintain your old Ford Ranger, because rather than make a car payment each month you want to put that cash toward your investments so you can meet your goal of retiring at fifty-five. That's a real "eyes on the prize" mentality.

If you look at your monthly statements and see that you're not saving nearly enough, it's time to ask yourself where your money is going. Are there lots of little things that don't *really* matter to you (how many streaming services do we really need?) that are preventing you from reaching your savings goals? Remember, "many a little makes a mickle."

MINDFUL INVESTING ACTIVITY

That was a lot of advice in one short chapter. Before moving on, let's do a check-in to see whether you're ready to begin investing. If you can't check off every box here, don't worry. This is just a way of creating a streamlined to-do list:

❏ Establish an emergency fund
❏ Eliminate high-interest debt
❏ Fall in love with compound interest
❏ Educate yourself about investing
❏ Know your "why"
❏ Have a plan
❏ Embrace your trade-offs

Note those items in your workbook and let that be your action plan for getting ready to invest. (Or, if you already have some investments, before you invest more. Remember, leaving those investments alone for a while isn't just okay — it's my number one recommendation!) Really think about each item before you move to the next one. The goal here is to get as financially fit as possible, not to rush through this exercise so that you can get to the fun part (that is, investing) more quickly. To return to Benjamin Franklin for a moment, don't forget one of his more commonly quoted aphorisms, "Haste makes waste."*

For a graphic that streamlines this advice (and more) into a flowchart, see appendix A.

---

* Benjamin Franklin, *Poor Richard's Almanack* (1758; repr., Waterloo, IA: USC Publishing Co., 1914), 24.

CHAPTER 7

Before You Hire an Adviser

No enemy is worse than bad advice.
— SOPHOCLES

Once you get to the point in your life where you're earning more money than you need to sustain yourself, you want to be sure you're managing your money safely and wisely. A quick internet search for "how to invest" will yield loads of ads for robo-advisers and tutorials for do-it-yourself investing. You'll see all the big brokers and plenty of independent registered investment advisers. At this point, it may be time to hire an adviser — or maybe you want to do it on your own. But if you *do* hire an adviser, it's important to understand what exactly this person can help you with, as well as the different types of fee structures out there.

As the way Wall Street works has shifted, so have advisers. Investment advice is no longer the commission-based system it once was. So how does it work now? Before we move further along the investment journey, let's talk about what type of financial advice will work best for you.

What Do Different Types of Advisers Do?

As we've stressed, the goal with your financial plan is to maintain a long-term outlook. Thus, if and when you hire a financial adviser, you'll want to have a long-term relationship with that person. A good financial adviser will help you to envision your future, create a personalized financial plan, and monitor that plan to make sure you're on track to achieve your goals. You'll always pay a fee for these services, of course, but the way different financial advisers' fees are charged and earned can be quite different. With some advisers, the fees are explicit and their work is transparent; with other advisers, not so much.

Some people opt to go the do-it-yourself route, which works great for those who enjoy doing financial planning and investment research and monitoring their portfolio. There are a lot of good online platforms out there to help you in this effort. For many people, though, the DIY path is too overwhelming, and they'd rather hire an adviser (I recommend an RIA) to support them. Some people go for a hybrid approach, meaning they use a digital planning tool for part of the process, and supplement the rest with human interaction, such as attending live Q&As with an adviser or hiring one who works on an hourly basis. To figure out what path will work best for you, it's important to first understand what you need to know.

Let's explore all our options.

The DIY Investor

I have a friend who *loves* cooking. He makes his own sauces, roasts beautiful cuts of meat, and serves each course with the right wine pairings. He uses tools like crème brûlée torches and mandolines. He will spend *hours* in the kitchen learning how to prepare each recipe flawlessly.

To me, that does not sound like fun. In fact, it sounds a lot like work. I'm not a cook; if you put me in charge of a meal, it will be simple and quick. And if you were to put that same kitchen wizard friend of mine behind a computer and ask him to spend a few hours managing his portfolio? He'd rather lose a finger on the cutting board.

To be your own adviser, you *must* take the time and energy to do it right, and it's important to enjoy the process, at least to some extent. If you don't, you're likely to put it off or not put in the effort the task requires, and you'll be more likely to make mistakes or to not do your finances justice. If you decide to be your own adviser, you'll first need to know which questions are important to ask and be willing to do your own research. We'll be going into more detail on these areas in the coming chapters, but in summary, you'll need to understand:

- what your financial goals are.
- what you are looking for and what you need to reach those financial goals.
- the whys and hows of asset allocation, diversification, and rebalancing.
- the differences between each asset class and how they behave.
- risk and how it functions in creating a long-term financial plan (more on that in the next chapter).
- how to reduce various risks with changes in your portfolio.
- how your taxes function in relation to your investments.

An important consideration here, again, is time. Most advisers will rebalance your portfolio quarterly, semiannually, or in response to certain market and economic factors.* They pay attention to what's going on in the markets and check in on your accounts as the markets zig and zag to make sure your allocations are still aligned with your goals. Then, advisers will buy or sell certain assets as needed to realign your accounts with your financial plan.

A Mindful Reminder

As with every stage of the financial-planning process, mindfulness is key. Being mindful of your own potential biases and blind spots can help you avoid emotional decision-making. Just as you may hire a therapist so that you have an unbiased individual to talk to, hiring a financial adviser means you have someone with enough emotional distance from your finances to help you to make the choices that are best for you. No emotions about it.

Keep the above in mind to help you decide whether you want to go this alone or have a guide along the path.

Robo-Advisers

As the name suggests, a robo-adviser provides financial management by way of an algorithm. The software is geared to a preset portfolio based on a questionnaire you fill out about your investment goals and risk tolerances. Since the process is automated, robo-advisers generally charge a lower annual management fee than human advisers would.

Most robo-advisers build portfolios using exchange-traded funds consisting of a blend of equities and bonds, depending

---

* Again, we go into lots of detail on rebalancing in chapter 12. For now, think "buy low, sell high."

on your risk tolerance and goals. Some also offer real estate exposure (via real estate investment trusts). The simpler your financial situation, the more likely a DIY or robo-adviser option may work for you. What you *don't* get with a robo-adviser is advice that is specifically tailored to your life and your goals.

What Human Advisers (Should) Do

Good advisers will start by asking about *you*. Where are you in your life? What are your short- and long-term goals? They'll ask questions like "When do you want to retire? What do you want your retirement to look like?" Good advisers will ask about what Morningstar calls "gamma" factors in retirement planning. This includes items like withdrawal rate, annuity purchase decisions, and tax efficiency. In fact, according to Morningstar, working with an adviser who helps you navigate these gamma factors can help you generate income levels more than 20 percent higher in retirement.* The more complex your financial situation (say you own one or more businesses), the more likely a financial adviser will be the right choice for you.

Good human financial advisers will help with different functions of money management, including the following crucial stages:

1. **Planning:** They will help you create a financial plan. Advisers will work with you to figure out your goals and understand your spending, then determine what asset allocation to use, which insurance policies to buy, and how much you should allocate to different goals each month.

---

* David Blanchett and Paul D. Kaplan, "The Value of a Gamma-Efficient Portfolio," Morningstar.com, October 25, 2017.

2. **Behavioral coaching:** Investing is emotional. Good advisers will coach you through the pitfalls associated with emotion-based decision-making. If you're tempted to sell when the markets dip, they'll talk you off that ledge and keep you on track, reminding you of your strategy and maintaining emotional detachment when you can't.

3. **Portfolio management:** Many advisers take on portfolio management, managing your investable assets (more on that in chapters to come).

4. **Wealth management:** Some advisers help you manage all aspects of your wealth, not just your investment portfolio. Wealth managers provide you with overall financial guidance, keep your finances on track, reduce your taxes, help you consider your legacy, and make sure all aspects of your financial world are working well together.

Great advisers will also help coordinate other professionals, such as the right estate planning attorneys, tax professionals, and business advisers.

How Financial Advisers Are Paid

If you decide to work with a financial adviser, it's important to understand how this person will be paid. You want to make sure you're getting good value for your money, whatever the level of service you need. Advisers are typically paid in one of three ways:

1. **Flat fee:** Some advisers charge a flat fee for specific services, such as creating a retirement plan or a college plan. Some robo-advisers charge a flat monthly or

retainer fee for services, rather than basing their fees on what your assets are worth.

2. **Assets under management (AUM):** This type of fee is a percentage of the assets you have under management. According to a 2018 study by industry consultants RIA in a Box, the average fee for adviser-driven portfolio management is 1.1 percent for clients with less than $250,000 and 0.7 percent for clients with over $5 million. Interestingly, total costs (inclusive of the cost of the investments themselves) was 1.3 percent for clients with less than $250,000 and 1.1 percent for clients with over $5 million.* Some advisers levy their fees in advance and some in arrears. Many robo-advisers also base their fees on your account balance, and since no human is investing time in your account the fees are lower (on average about 0.25 percent annually). If you decide to use a human or robo-adviser that charges AUM fees, you must make sure you're getting your money's worth. The advisory fee can be one of a client's largest annual fees, and you have to look at the cost to you as not only the fee itself but also all the potential compounding that you will be losing by paying it. To be worth it, your adviser had better do more than "manage investments." Don't know where to start in assessing this? I've created a free online tool to help you make the right choice for your needs (more about that at the end of this chapter).

3. **Commissions:** Back in the '90s and for many years proceeding, brokers were all paid by commission. Regardless of whether clients' net worth increased or

---

*   "2018 RIA Industry Study: Average Investment Advisory Fee is 0.95%," *RIA in a Box* (blog), June 18, 2018, riainabox.com.

decreased, brokers received a commission for every
product they sold. While most basic investments are
offered without commissions these days, there are investments (insurance products and private equity deals
to name two) that still have commissions associated
with them. It's buyer beware in these spaces, just like
in the not-always-so-good old days.

If you go with a human adviser, the most important factor in
choosing the right individual is trustworthiness. Much as you
probably wouldn't leave your child or pet with a sitter you
don't know and trust, you wouldn't leave your money in the
hands of someone who doesn't give you a good feeling, right?

What Is a Fiduciary and
Why Do You Need One?

Most of us have seen those people at the stands in the mall
selling hair products or cellphone accessories, and we certainly
all get telemarketer calls. Do we trust these people when they
say they've got the best deal for us right now? Will we refi-
nance our car with them, try this new pomade, or buy their
solar panels?* Usually not. Why? Because that salesperson is
probably just some guy in a call center trying to sell as many
solar panels as he can by lunchtime. He doesn't care about
your home or your electricity bills; maybe he doesn't even care
about global warming. What does he care about? His commissions. Why would you go with a financial adviser who very
well may be thinking the same way? Sure, we're not back in the
days of the "Wolf of Wall Street" Jordan Belfort and the industry doesn't work the way it used to. But when working with

---

* This is in no way a dis on solar panels. They're great.

advisers whose payment structure is based on commissions, it's hard to tell when they're recommending something because it's right for you and when it's because they know they'll make some extra cash. As Upton Sinclair said, "It is difficult to get a man to understand something when his salary depends on his not understanding it."*

One way to reduce the chance that you'll end up with a financial adviser who has a conflict of interest is to look for fiduciaries, who are financial professionals required by law to put your interests above theirs. This applies to advisers who receive some form of commission too. Fiduciaries are required to steer you toward any products or investments that will benefit your portfolio, even if it means a lower commission for them. Choosing a fiduciary is one of the most important ways you can protect yourself when working with an adviser.

Choosing the Right Adviser: Green Flags and Red

If and when you decide to start working with a financial adviser, it's important to look out for both red flags and green ones. Some signs that your adviser is a good fit?

1. They ask questions.
2. They have a clear fee schedule.
3. They explain their investment strategy in simple language.
4. They offer a written agreement.

This is important stuff. Any good adviser should display all the green flags and none of the red ones.

---

* Upton Sinclair, *I, Candidate for Governor: And How I Got Licked* (1935; repr., Berkeley: University of California Press, 1994), 109.

GREEN FLAGS	RED FLAGS
The adviser seeks to understand your situation, goals, and needs before getting started.	Any adviser who pushes products before even learning your story.
The adviser is transparent about their fees and helps you understand what you're paying for. There might be tiers based on account size, but a good adviser will make that clear from the start.	Unusual fees attached to certain investments. For example, there might be additional costs associated with hedge funds or exotic investments (such as private equity, venture capital, leveraged buyout, seed funding, or global macro, to name a few).
The adviser can explain their investment strategy, tell you how they'll manage your funds, and what principles inform their decisions.	Any adviser who can't give you a clear description of their investment strategy or philosophy.
They are willing to put their terms in writing and are available to answer questions before taking any action on your behalf.	Any adviser who claims to be a fiduciary but will not put that statement, or their fee structure, in writing.

My Investing Philosophy

My investment philosophy is simple. Start with the assumption that we, as global citizens, are always trying to improve our lot in life. We all want to live more fully, become the best versions of ourselves, enjoy our lives, provide for our families, and leave the world (or at least our small corner of it) a little better than before we arrived. There are more of us than ever, we are living longer than ever, and our collective brilliance creates an exponential curve of progress. Business does an incredible job of organizing the innovative and productive resources of the world toward providing the goods and services that make these things possible. Even when the government spends on something — roads, school construction, healthcare — it is often for-profit companies that do the actual work. This is why I believe in the long-term benefits of owning shares of the great companies in both the United States and the wider world.

For most of my invested capital (90 percent), I invest in a broadly diversified global equity portfolio. A little more than half of the global market capitalization* is found in the United States, so I invest about half of my portfolio here. This means that the other half is invested internationally — about one-fourth to one-third in emerging markets and the rest (two-thirds to three-fourths) in the developed world outside the United States. Ideally, I would recommend you own the most broadly available index in each of these three types of market available at the time, for the lowest cost.

When you invest in an index, you are not investing equal sums into each of the companies within the index. Instead, each index is organized to "weight" some companies more heavily than other companies. Most well-known indices are capitalization-weighted. "Capitalization" refers to the total value or size of the company (number of shares multiplied by the price per share). When you have a capitalization-weighted index, the weighting decision is based on the size of the company.

---

*   Market capitalization, or "market cap," is the total market value of a company's outstanding shares of stock. This figure allows investors to appraise a company based on how valuable the public perceives it to be. More on this in the upcoming chapters.

Consider the best-known example of a capitalization-weighted index, the S&P 500. When you invest in the S&P 500, you are not splitting your investment up equally among the five hundred (or so) companies; you are buying an amount of each company that represents its relative size or weighting within the index. This means you are buying more of the largest companies and less of the smallest companies — 7 percent Apple, 6 percent Microsoft, 2.6 percent Amazon, all the way down to 0.006 percent for DISH Network and NewsCorp. This is normal index construction and there is nothing wrong with it ... most people do it this way. I would recommend this as where you should start.

But this is not exactly what I do. As it happens, I discovered the academic research of Eugene Fama and Kenneth French and their five-factor model that considers size, value, quality, profitability, and investment pattern in portfolio weighting.* I invest my portfolios into funds and ETFs that incorporate these factors, tilting my ownership of the great companies toward valuation, small-cap, and profitability, instead of concentrating on owning more of the biggest companies. This means my portfolios cost a little more and behave a little differently than a pure capitalization-weighted index.

I use factors in my personal portfolios because I believe they will outperform (as the historical research suggests), but there is no guarantee this will happen. I am okay with this difference, even though it can be frustrating when I underperform the index. I hold on through the frustration because my belief in better long-term outcomes is strong. If my belief weakens, I will fall back to pure index investing and keep my costs as low as I possibly can. For most people (especially those for whom the last

---

*   Eugene F. Fama and Kenneth R. French, "A Five-Factor Asset Pricing Model," Fama-Miller working paper, September 2014, doi.org /10.2139/ssrn.2287202.

couple paragraphs were too much "finance speak"), I would recommend keeping it simple and sticking with the combination
of good ol' capitalization weighting and lowest possible cost —
an excellent way to invest. For the rest of my invested capital,
I own private businesses either directly or through angel/seed
funding (private equity) vehicles. I do not believe that I have
any special expertise in this space, and I have not experienced
anything like above-average returns from my seed investments.
I do it because I *love* entrepreneurship and investing in business
owners. I also know how unlikely it is I will be successful at this
very high-risk category of investing, so I limit my exposure to it.
I believe I will have a better outcome than if I were gambling;
but if not, it will still have been worth it for the joy I get from
talking to these entrepreneurs.

For even more detail on how I invest, see appendix C.

Now that we've explored the mindset of investing and understand the shape our accounts should be in *before* we start
investing, it's time for the fun stuff: *how* to invest. Where do
we put our money and how much do we divvy up into each
asset type? In the next chapter, we'll start by understanding the
relationship between risk and return.

MINDFUL INVESTING ACTIVITY

As we move into the next chapters about *how* to invest,
keep in mind whether you want to go down the investing road by yourself, you want to hire an adviser in some
capacity, or you prefer to enlist the aid of robo-advisers.
Before you get too far into the process of interviewing
potential advisers (or checking out DIY options), figure
out whether a given professional will be best for your
needs. On my website, at mindful.money/resources,

you'll find my "Long-Term Cost of Hiring a Financial Advisor Calculator," where you can enter relevant facts and figures regarding your current situation, projected fees and earnings, and the rather shocking amount of compound interest you'd miss out on over the decades. Still, the right adviser might be worth it to you for any number of reasons. The questions below — ten for any potential adviser, three for yourself — will help you with this process.

Questions to Ask a Potential Adviser

1. Are you a fiduciary?
2. What are your credentials? Are they up to date?
3. What type of experience do you have?
4. Do you have any disciplinary actions on your record?
5. How are you paid?
6. How do you report investment performance?
7. What does my fee include?
8. What is your investment philosophy?
9. Where will you keep my assets?
10. How often will we meet?

Questions to Ask Yourself

1. How much time am I willing and able to put into personal financial planning and investing research?
2. Do I *like* thinking about money and investing? Will I make enough time to learn about it?
3. Can I stay mindful on my own? Will I benefit from having someone help me stick mindfully to my plan?

CHAPTER 8

The Risk/Return
Relationship

Danger and delight grow on one stalk.
— ENGLISH PROVERB

If you remember only one thing from this book, it should be that investing is the only way to generate enough income to last you throughout retirement, and that savings alone will not get you there unless you are very, very wealthy. So why are so many people hesitant to invest? The risk. Or rather, what we *perceive* as risk.

Humans are wired to avoid risk. When we see potential threats, our senses heighten and we have a gut reaction. Back in the days of the Neanderthal, that worked for us. *Me see saber-tooth, me run.* But in modern times, we must adapt to modern threats. Our investment portfolios are a great example. Not only should we mindfully stick with our investments (i.e., not panic and sell when the market drops), we should make our initial investment choices based on the potential for long-term return, not the risk of short-term loss.

How an Aversion to Risk Is
an Aversion to Return

In chapter 5 we touched on Kahneman and Tversky's prospect theory, which says that investors tend to put more weight on losses than they do on gains. An individual presented with two portfolio options — one promising a steady gain of 5 percent over thirty years versus another with a 10 percent return over thirty years but some 50 percent dips along the way — is more likely to go with the first option even though the second will be more profitable in the long run. Humans are wired to gravitate toward safety. But avoiding what we perceive as risk is actively damaging to our long-term portfolios.

In terms of assets, people who are more averse to risk tend to favor a portfolio blend with fewer equities and more bonds. Bonds feel like a much safer bet in terms of what they will provide: a set return amount over a specified period. We know what we're getting into, and it feels safe. However, the return on bonds is significantly lower than the potential return on equities. And what we've proven repeatedly is that in the long term (ten, twenty, thirty years), equities always outperform bonds, hands down.

When it's time to talk asset allocation (stay tuned for chapter 9) we'll look at what kind of equity blend we're talking about here. But in a nutshell, you must have a diversified equity distribution in your portfolio if you want to see higher returns in the long term.

So we know that the rate of return for equities is significantly higher than it is for bonds, and we already know that keeping cash in a straight-up savings account means you are losing money over time because the returns are so low while inflation creeps ever upward. Still, we are often afraid to put too much of our money into equities. This is where we need to zoom out and look at the big picture.

Managing the Gut Reaction

If you have a general bias toward investing in bonds, your portfolio will not perform well enough to meet your long-term needs. If your bias is toward avoiding risk and you *do* invest in equities, you'll be tempted to get out the moment the market goes down. It is crucial to be aware of that gut reaction and the resulting knee-jerk decision. Everyone responds that way — we're human! The important thing is to be mindful of that reaction so that we don't make any sudden, unplanned choices and stray from the plan we made at the start, when the market wasn't so chaotic and things didn't feel as risky. Again, a long-term outlook is key.

Remember that graph from chapter 5 that showed the market's ups and downs over a hundred-plus-year period? To understand how stocks perform, we cannot look at a period of one day, one month, or even one year. We *must* look at the bigger picture. When you need a reminder, look at a ten-, twenty-, or thirty-year segment of the market from any given time and focus on all that growth. Zigs and zags will happen and it's fine to notice them, but it's critically important to stick with your plan.

The Risk-Tolerant versus Risk-Averse Investor

Say I wake up on a Tuesday morning and my wife gives me a kiss, my daughter runs in to give me a hug as I get out of bed, the cat saunters by and wants a belly rub, breakfast is already made — a great start to the day! I'll probably be very risk tolerant all day. I'll feel good about risk because nothing feels particularly *at* risk; things seem good and my outlook is positive.

However, when things aren't going as well, we tend to be more risk averse. A few weeks after my brother died, I was nervously waiting to hear that my son Eli's flight from San Francisco had landed safely in New York. During those same fretful hours, my daughter Annie texted to tell me she was heading to the beach with a friend. The combination of these circumstances sent me over the edge that day. I had an immediate, intense reaction to Annie's text. My brother had died by drowning. The thought of my daughter going out into the ocean only a couple of months later felt like an incredible risk and I could not deal with it. I broke down and cried because my anxiety around my daughter's safety was too much for me to take. I knew this was irrational fear, so I accepted the risk and let her go. Annie had a great time at the beach that day and was never aware of my worry.

My fear of potentially losing one of my kids — because I'd had that recent loss of my brother — was monumental. When I got the text from Annie that afternoon, the idea that her life could be at risk was more than I could handle; because of recent events in my life I reacted in a way that I normally would not. That is an extreme example of something that's very human, but the fact is that we behave similarly when markets suffer big losses. When the market is volatile and we see that our accounts are down, we don't like that, and our gut reaction is to want to get out of it.

That is prospect theory at work. We tend to put more weight on potential loss than we do on potential gain. Risk tolerance is an attempt at quantifying the reality that some loss will happen while maintaining an "eyes on the prize" mentality — the prize in this case being that strong likelihood of future gain.

When I'm working with a client, I want their portfolio to include just enough bonds that they will hold on to it when its value goes down. I know that it will go down at some point, I *tell* them it will go down at some point, and I want to get a good sense of how much it can go down before they lose sleep, panic, and sell. So I try to go right to the edge of that comfort zone and not tip over it.

The big challenge in asking the question about someone's risk tolerance is that it's different not just for every person, but every day. There are plenty of companies out there that have questionnaires to assess your risk tolerance and assign you a score, which I think is total crap. Risk tolerance is not something you can measure. That's like asking someone how they will respond to a horrific event. If someone had asked you in the year 1999, "How would you respond if terrorists flew commercial airliners into the World Trade Center?" you would have had no clue. You wouldn't necessarily think about the buildings falling, the fires, the people falling to their deaths, or how long the event would be present in your mind and that of the country at large.

The same goes for any loss. I could never have guessed how the death of my brother would affect me until it happened. There is no way. Over the years I've talked to many friends and clients who have lost parents, children, and siblings. I felt for them and tried to understand their pain. But I now understand that the knowledge of someone else going through something is not in any way the same as going through it yourself. The same is true for markets. You can read every book and watch every documentary about the Great Depression, but it still could never really tell you what it was like to live through it or to know what choices you might have made for your finances and your family.

The beauty of creating a financial plan is that you don't have to worry about what you'll do when losses happen — because your plan will be to sit mindfully and do *nothing*. Investing wisely and mindfully is simple. The difficult part is managing our emotions and impulses.

How Your Risk Tolerance Can Affect Your Asset Allocation

Risk tolerance cannot be the driver of how you organize your portfolio. It's an input, but it's not the driver. When you're making a financial plan, you have to accept trade-offs. You must decide which things are most important to you among factors that may include when you want to retire and what your ideal retirement looks like, how you might support your children or other family members, how much of a cushion you might need to support your parents, and even how often you might want to take a nice vacation. Once you've got those factors determined, how much money you will need is a quantifiable thing, and you can make your plan around whatever those numbers end up being. Once you quantify your goals and understand how much you need to set aside, there is usually a trade-off. Most people can't "have it all," in this case meaning the spending habits, the early retirement, the big vacations, plus the cushy savings accounts. We need to make trade-offs to reach the most important goals. Maybe you save more so you can retire earlier; maybe you spend more knowing that you'll have to retire later to make it work. But if you're able to invest early and for the long term, you'll be able to accommodate more of your lifestyle goals and the trade-offs will be less extreme.

Some people are reluctant to take investment risks even when their monetary gain will be higher in the long term. We see this a lot with folks who are older (who may need to use their retirement money sooner, or already *are* using that money) and with folks who are wealthier and afraid to lose what they have. This isn't necessarily a bad thing; if you have plenty of money to last your lifetime and feel better knowing the exact amount that will be available, with no potential for dips, that's a completely fine choice too.

The folks who really need to be mindful of risk aversion are those who, according to their lifestyle values and goals, *should* be investing more of their portfolios in equities but who may not have a mindful market outlook. This aversion to risk means that the person is prone to making investments that have a low uncertainty — meaning that they can be fairly sure what their returns will be. Again, bonds are a great example of this. Since they provide a secure return amount to be paid at a specified time (barring unforeseen, unlikely failures like, say, bankruptcy or government collapse), bonds feel much less risky. The problem with investing mostly in bonds is that their payout is *much* lower than the payout we see with equities.

That is why it is crucial to create an asset-allocation blend that will have enough equities to produce the return you need to reach your retirement and other financial goals. So how do you know how to divvy up your portfolio? Let's talk asset allocation.

MINDFUL INVESTING ACTIVITY

You have to always remember that humans are wired to avoid risk — an instinct that served us well through our evolution but can harm us in our complicated modern world. Our odds of being eaten by a lion today are basically nil, but the instincts we evolved to avoid such a fate can still take over if we don't learn to recognize and resist them.

If you don't already make time for a mindfulness practice in your everyday life, you may find that even five minutes a day of meditation will help. An app like Headspace is a great beginner's resource, with guided exercises ranging from five to twenty or more minutes, for general stress relief and the calming of anxiety, as well as more targeted topics like mindful budgeting and spending, handling financial stress, and much more.

But it is not just about feeling better. Meditation creates a functional difference. What you are trying to accomplish through meditation is to increase the space between an experience and your reaction to the experience. This will benefit many different areas of your life, and for our purposes imagine being nonreactive in the face of a falling market. If you can better manage your emotional response, you can better manage your actual response. Investors make their money in times of high stress. You can feel your feelings, but as Warren Buffett said in the 1986 Berkshire Hathaway shareholder letter, "We simply attempt to be fearful when others are greedy and to be greedy only when others are fearful."

As a reminder, rewrite the text below in your notebook in big, bold letters. When you're feeling shaky, flip to that page and take a moment of mindful calm to absorb these simple facts all over again.

What's *actually* risky:

1. Not investing at all.
2. Buying individual stocks.

If you're still feeling overwhelmed and like you might make a financial decision you'll regret, don't hesitate to call your adviser (if you have one) or even a trusted friend or family member, and let them talk you down.

CHAPTER 9

Plan-Appropriate
Asset Allocation

The means prepare the end,
and the end is what the means have made it.
— JOHN MORLEY

If you were to make a delicious old-school lasagna, you'd need two components: plenty of time and the right ingredients. Can you whip up a quick version of lasagna with a jar of sauce, a block of mozzarella, and some noodles? Sure. But it won't be the same as if you were to spend all afternoon in the kitchen simmering a homemade sauce with fresh tomatoes and basil from the garden, a nice Italian sausage, and a blend of mozzarella, ricotta, and parmesan to give it that perfect combination of texture and taste. The same concept applies to choosing the right blend of components for your investment portfolio: the right ratio of assets makes a major impact on the returns, the volatility, and the access to liquidity when it is needed.

Much as a recipe is your plan for cooking a meal, asset allocation is your plan for organizing your investments; that is, what percentage of your assets you'll allocate to cash, to bonds, and to equities.

Each of these asset classes has different risks and returns, so how you allocate funds (and whether you can maintain that allocation in the face of short-term setbacks) will largely determine what returns you'll see in the long term. The goal is to understand how much money you'll need overall, then divide your funds between the three asset classes in a way that will give you the returns you need to reach that goal.

The key to determining your ideal asset allocation is to balance risk and reward based on your financial goals, your risk tolerance, and your time frame. You can plug these metrics into almost any investing website (E*TRADE, Vanguard, Charles Schwab, etc.) and get a simple pie chart that shows what your asset allocation might look like. See figure 5.

The key to smart asset allocation is understanding where you fit on the scale from moderate to aggressive and what returns you'll need to meet your goals, and then dividing your funds among the three asset classes accordingly. Stick with your plan and give it time — in other words, don't change the recipe midway through the process!

The Return on Cash

As we've already explored, the return on cash is far lower than on any other asset class. Assuming you're not saving your cash under your mattress, in a safe in the crawl space, or buried in your yard (don't do that), the returns you'd see on, say, a money market account are typically about 2 to 3 percent. Given that inflation averages about 3 percent, there's no way a cash-only retirement plan will provide you with the funds you need once your current income stops coming in.

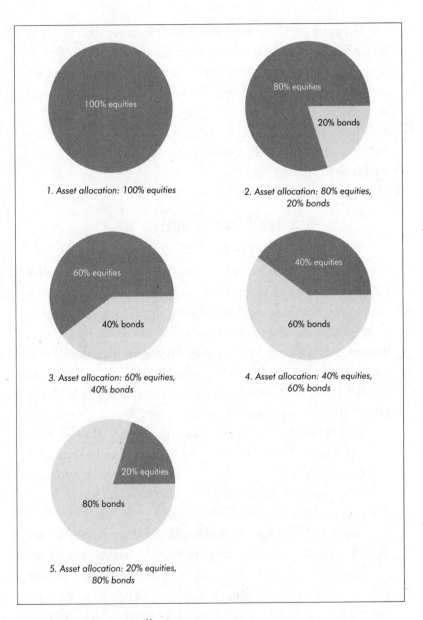

1. Asset allocation: 100% equities

2. Asset allocation: 80% equities, 20% bonds

3. Asset allocation: 60% equities, 40% bonds

4. Asset allocation: 40% equities, 60% bonds

5. Asset allocation: 20% equities, 80% bonds

Figure 5. Five asset allocations

The reason to keep any cash at all is because you expect to spend it, either sometime soon or in the unpredictable future. Remember that emergency fund we talked about having set up *before* you start investing? That's a fund you always want to keep on hand. The last thing you want to have to do is pull from your portfolio if markets are down at the precise moment that your refrigerator (or something bigger) needs repairing (or replacing).

Bonds: When Stability Isn't Always the Best Thing

Bonds are called fixed income securities for a reason: they offer a specific return you can rely on. That number is fixed and the chance you would lose principal is minimal. One could make an argument that bonds have always been a good investment because interest rates have been in decline for decades. If you buy a bond now, you're getting a locked-in rate, and chances are that a couple of years from now interest rates will be down even further — so lock in those rates now. Right?

Well, interest rates are *not* always in decline. They eventually trend up, come back down, go up again, and so on. The real reason you'd want to have bonds is for ballast, and that ballast is to keep you invested when everything in your body is saying you should sell.

The issue with having too much of your portfolio anchored in fixed income assets is that "fixed" part. Bonds are set at a fixed return amount that is simply too low to keep up with inflation. According to Vanguard, between 1926 and 2019 the average rate of return on bonds was 5.33 percent.* The average

---

*   "Portfolio Allocations: Historical Index Risk/Return (1926–2019),"
       Vanguard, n.d., advisors.vanguard.com.

rate of return on equities during this same period was 10.29 percent. To go with an extreme hypothetical here, if you were to keep all your assets in bonds, you would see around half the returns as if you had kept all your assets in equities. But it doesn't end there. These figures reflect the nominal returns — that is, before inflation is taken into account. The difference in those return rates gets even more significant once we factor in an inflation rate of 3 percent:

- 5.33% (return on bonds) – 3% (inflation) = 2.33%.
- 10.29% (return on equities) – 3% (inflation) = 7.29%.

What further affects these returns is our good ol' friend taxes. Fixed income returns (meaning bonds) are considered at least partially income and are taxed as such. However, stock returns are mostly classified as capital gains (profits from the sale of assets) and are thus taxed at lower rates. Advantage, equities!

If you had decided to keep 100 percent of your assets in equities, however, you'd have to prepare yourself for a 50 percent decline every so often throughout the life of those investments. You must be able to stomach that idea, hold on, and wait until things come back up again — and that could take months or years. A lot of people have a hard time doing that, which is okay. The important thing is to understand how the markets work, how much zigging and zagging you can tolerate, and to plan accordingly.

Again, we're talking long term. Over extended periods of time, equities outperform bonds. Over any short period, it's anybody's guess which will do better. But in a lifetime of planning and investing, equities are going to provide the bulk of your return.

Equity Overview

A well-balanced portfolio should have a diverse blend of equities. We'll go into more detail on the various types of equity in chapter 11 on diversification, but let's take a high-level overview here.

First, it's important to have a basic understanding of market capitalization, which in a nutshell means how much a company is worth. Market cap is the total value of a company's outstanding shares of stock, which essentially means the number of shares of company stock held by all its shareholders multiplied by the price of each individual share. Capitalization is purely the market value of a company, which, for those of us who trust market prices, is probably the best measure of size.

It's also important to note that these distinctions aren't perfect. In some cases, share prices may be considered by some to be overvalued. For example, as I write this in 2023, Tesla's market cap is $620 billion (even after a huge decline in the company's stock price), while Ford is valued at about $50 billion. Shares of Tesla are so incredibly high because people *believe* them to be worth so much more than everybody else, including Ford — a company that's been successfully building vehicles for over one hundred years, far longer than Tesla.

In an upcoming chapter we'll look at why each type of equity produces the returns it does (and why it's important to have a diverse collection of all these subsets in your portfolio). For now, here's an overview of the different types of equities we'll be referencing:

- **Large-cap stocks:** These are shares issued by companies with a market cap over $10 billion, some of the largest US companies.
- **Mid-cap stocks:** Shares of companies with a market cap between $2 billion and $10 billion.

- **Small-cap stocks:** These are from companies with a market cap of less than $2 billion.
- **International investments:** Describes any stocks from companies outside the United States, which you can buy via a foreign exchange or within a fund.
- **Emerging markets:** Stocks from companies based in developing nations, such as India, Brazil, Mexico, or Pakistan. Most of these stocks are seen as much higher risk but have the potential for much higher reward. (We'll go into more detail in chapter 11 on *why* emerging markets are riskier investments.)
- **Exotic investments:** Describes atypical investments such as private equity (PV), venture capital (VC), leveraged buyout (LBO), and seed funding. These have the potential for big returns... and big losses. (I do not recommend investing in exotic markets unless you have a lot of funds to play with and can handle the potential losses. We'll explore each of these markets more in chapter 11.)
- **Real estate investment trusts:** These are not technically stocks, but you can buy a publicly traded REIT just like a stock on the stock exchange. A REIT is an investment in the asset value and income-producing capacity of real estate equity. (This is another investment tool I don't recommend for most, which we'll discuss in chapter 15.)

How Many Equities Are We Talking About Here?

The key ingredients in any strong investment portfolio are asset allocation, diversification, and rebalancing. That diversification piece cannot be stressed enough. Diversify, diversify,

diversify! This isn't a new concept, but it *is* one that many people forget to account for when the pundits are pushing for this or that new stock.

We're going to spend a whole chapter on diversification, but a quick word here. When we talk about diversification within equities, there are several factors to consider, mainly company size (market cap), industry or sector, and geographic location. It's important to have a massive, diverse blend of each subset of equities so that when one dips down or completely crashes, you'll be okay. In the event of downturns in one field, you will have an array of other equities to rely on; if you're well diversified, they're not all going to go down at once. Diversification means stabilization. And when the *entire* market does dip — which it will — the best course of action is the simplest: to wait patiently for it to recover (which it will).

I want to reiterate that I never recommend buying individual stocks. Talk about risk! Sure, you can win big if that one stock does well, but it's far too much like putting one big chip down on the roulette table and hoping your number will come up. There is nothing that you can (legally) know that the market doesn't already know. There is no edge to be had when it comes to stock selection — there are just a lot of people making guesses, a few of which will be right (read: lucky). If you're spreading smaller chips across all the numbers, you'll be okay no matter where the wheel stops.

So how do you own a bit of everything if you're not buying individual stocks? Pooled investments.

For peace of mind, you want to invest in funds that inspire confidence because they are so broadly diverse. When I say broadly, I'm not talking about buying ten stocks or twenty. I'm talking about hundreds or thousands. Own it all! And since we're not billionaires who can afford to buy enough individual shares to make it worth the risk/reward ratio, we buy funds that are made up of slivers of hundreds or thousands of companies, depending on which fund you buy. There are three main fund types:

- **Mutual funds:** These funds comprise a selected group of stocks that are actively managed, which means there is a slightly higher chance of a better return, but there's also a slightly higher fee associated with them. Mutual funds can be bought and sold at market close.
- **Index funds:** These are funds comprising a selected group of stocks that are passively managed, meaning no person is actively watching these accounts. They tend to perform better over the long haul than actively managed mutual funds, and their fees are lower since no human is on the clock overseeing them.
- **Exchange-traded funds:** These function in essentially the same way as mutual funds and index funds, but investors can buy much smaller pieces of the pie. ETFs are bought and sold like stocks (they have a ticker number and everything). Since ETFs are not a fund, there is no minimum purchase amount, making them more widely accessible to people who might not have as deep a pocket to pull from.

Again, the central idea is *simplicity*. You want to buy a diverse portfolio and then not touch it (except during your annual rebalance, which we'll talk more about in chapter 12). But for now, keep in mind that your investments should be "set it and forget it" — for twenty, thirty, forty, fifty, or more years.

An Aside on Funds

The Russell 3000 is an index that contains the largest three thousand publicly traded companies in the United States; it tries to be the benchmark for the entire US market. When you buy into one of these funds, you're buying the equivalent of tiny slivers of those three thousand companies. These funds are strategically divided among each company type depending on their market capitalizations; a higher percentage of the fund is allocated toward the larger companies, a smaller percentage for the smaller ones.

As another example, take the Vanguard Total Stock Market Index Fund (VTSAX). This is a broadly diversified fund made up of 4,124 stocks, representing 4,124 companies. Now *that* is broad diversification. This fund's top ten holdings take up 23.69 percent of the pool's total assets. These top ten are the big players, companies like Microsoft, Apple, Amazon, Google, Tesla, Facebook, and the like. The other 76.31 percent is divided up between the four thousand or so other companies. Therefore, while this fund is composed of 1.8 percent Tesla, it might also contain, say, 0.05 percent of Walgreens or Walmart and many others. This means that you're still able to see the potential gains of the tech giants, but you don't have to guess which ones will do well, which ones will *continue* to do well, and which other companies outside of tech are going to do well.

Remember Pokémon's catchphrase, "Gotta catch 'em all"? Well with businesses, you gotta own 'em all. The beauty of this type of broad diversification is that it allows you to consistently look at the big picture because you are capturing the *entire* market. Market leadership changes over time, and no one has been consistently able to predict future winners over a decades-long period. Understanding this is vital to the success of your portfolio. Recall again that graph of the last hundred-plus years of the US stock market; take any thirty-year chunk and you'll see that the overall growth of the entire market was up. Don't pay attention to those dips — zoom out and look at the upward line. If you own tiny pieces of the entire market, your portfolio will follow that same trajectory.

Welcome to Boring

Think about any movie that involves Wall Street and you'll see the suited people down there on the floor, heads in their hands when the numbers go down or ecstatically, almost frantically raising a glass and lighting a cigar when things skyrocket. It's a lot of up and down, excitement on one end and devastation on the other.

The thing is that if you want to be successful and make money long term, your portfolio and thus your day-to-day (and year-to-year) experience should be pretty boring. Buy your broadly diversified funds then don't pay attention to all the possibilities of what's going on in the global economy. Just think boring. Allow me to explain.

In 2020, we saw surges in certain stocks and major drops in others. Take Peloton, the home exercise–system company. People wanted to stay or get fit during the pandemic lockdowns, so they were buying home gyms. Peloton's shares climbed from about $25 per share prepandemic to $150 per share by January 2021.

If you'd been in on that stock's climb, you could have made a pretty penny. But as often happens in the market, what goes quickly up can come quickly down. Once the vaccine became available, consumers predicted that folks would be raring to get out of the house and back into the gym. Within weeks of vaccination rollouts, Peloton stocks began their descent back down the hill, where they ended 2021 at around $35 per share.

There are many examples of stocks soaring up and shooting back down. You might have kicked yourself for not getting in on the Peloton gain, but how were you supposed to know when and why their shares might soar and when they might come down again? That's the thing. You can't. It's impossible to know. There are a lot of other things you could be doing with your time than checking your portfolio every day wondering when to buy, when to sell, and which pundit to trust.

If you own a little bit of everything, your portfolio will go up over time. If you own shares of the companies that are soaring, you'll make money; if you own shares of companies whose stock values are dropping, you'll lose money. The trick is to own it all so that no single losing ticker brings your portfolio too far down. The goal is for your entire portfolio to slowly climb the hill over a long period. Think about the tortoise and the hare and remember who wins in that story.

Sure, it's boring. You buy your broadly diversified funds and don't even look at them except once or twice a year to rebalance, and that's it. For decades. You don't really have to do more than that. No incredibly monumental gains, but no incredibly monumental losses. Boring, but effective.

Simplify, Simplify, Simplify!

As I write this, I am fifty-one years old. I won't retire for another ten or fifteen years, which means that I will not need to rely on my investments until then. My personal portfolio is 100 percent equities, with some cash. I don't invest in bonds. I have an income stream and I don't need to rely on my investments. I'm going to let them cook for a long time. And I know that, because I'm 100 percent invested in equities, I'll be seeing about a 10 percent average payout on my investments over the life of my portfolio. That's a pretty large return.

I'm planning on about forty or so years of needing that retirement money, which is a long time! That's why my portfolio is all equities — I need to know that its value will climb consistently so as to make me enough money to last me into retirement and hopefully to leave a significant sum behind for my family and the causes I care about when I'm gone. I'm not recommending everyone go 100 percent equities,* but if you can deal with volatility, equities will be a much better driver of return. It's like that classic lasagna. You find the recipe you want, add all those fresh herbs, and let the sauce simmer for a few hours until you get that exceptional flavor. But you must follow the recipe.

Create your financial plan so you know what returns you'll need, allocate your assets into a broadly diversified portfolio with plenty of stocks, then let it cook for a few decades. Yes, you'll need to stir the sauce occasionally, to rebalance the flavors, but otherwise the biggest factor to take into account is time. Simple.

MINDFUL INVESTING ACTIVITY

As we discussed at the beginning of this chapter, the key to determining your ideal asset allocation is to balance risk and reward based on your financial goals, your risk tolerance, and your time frame.

As you no doubt have gathered by now, I will always propose a relatively high proportion of stocks to

---

*   I repeat: this is *not* a recommendation. I don't know you (the reader) or your needs; I do, however, know and love the power of diversified equities.

bonds — 100/0 in my case, but that's what works for me, based on my balance of these factors.

To get a sense of your ideal asset allocation, make use of the tools available online at any of the major investing websites (E*TRADE, Vanguard, Charles Schwab, etc.). You can try out any number of potential scenarios and get a simple pie chart that shows what your asset allocation might look like in a variety of allocation ratios.

If you feel stuck between the returns you want or need for your long-term planning and your current risk tolerance, these visuals can really help put the trade-offs in perspective. If it still seems overwhelming, or you're having a hard time getting past a fear of volatility, start by revisiting the Mindful Investing Activity you did in chapter 8 (you *did* do it, right?) for a sense of perspective. If you *still* feel stuck, it may be time to call in a professional to help walk you through these options and give you the confidence to get a little bit outside your low-return comfort zone!

What to Expect
When You're Investing

Blessed is he who expects nothing,
for he shall never be disappointed.
— ALEXANDER POPE

A friend of mine has a cattle dog. That dog will sprint around the yard, take hours-long hikes, and wear out any other playmates at the dog park. She'll get home and pass out on her dog bed for the rest of the afternoon and all the way until the next morning. There's nothing you can do to rouse her at that point. She is *beat*. But guess what? You take her out again the next morning and she'll do the exact same yard sprint, hike, or dog park routine as if yesterday never happened. A good night's rest and she's a brand-new dog! All she needed was a little time to recover. Same goes for markets. They can spiral downward and might look like they're crashed and going to stay crashed; but give them some time to recover and they'll be back where they were before and ready to climb even higher. Keep this in mind as we explore realistic expectations for returns.

Realistic Return Expectations

When making your investment plan, it's important to understand your *entire* financial situation. How much do you have saved already? How much can you realistically continue to save and add to your portfolio to achieve your goals — including when and how you'd like to retire? The first step in understanding how to allocate the assets in your investment portfolio is to understand what kinds of returns you can realistically expect based on your allocation choices.

Remember those asset-allocation pie charts from chapter 9? Each of these bond-to-equity blends gives a different but predictable return over the long term. The easiest way to understand return expectations is to first look at the extremes at either end. According to data compiled by NYU Stern School of Business professor Aswath Damodaran, a portfolio that is 100 percent bonds has seen an average annual return of almost 5 percent between 1928 and 2022, while a portfolio that is 100 percent equities has seen an average return of about 11 percent over the same time period.*

Of course, there are lots of different blends you can choose — 60/40 percent equities to bonds, 10/90 percent equities to bonds, a 50/50 split. Before deciding what's right for you, it's important to understand three things:

1. How much money you will need to meet your financial goals.
2. How much risk you're willing to take on and how capable you are of weathering drops in the market.
3. What types of returns you should expect to see based on your asset allocation.

---

* Aswath Damodaran, "Historical Returns on Stocks, Bonds and Bills: 1928–2022," NYU Stern School of Business, January 2023, https://pages .stern.nyu.edu/~adamodar/New_Home_Page/datafile/histretSP.html.

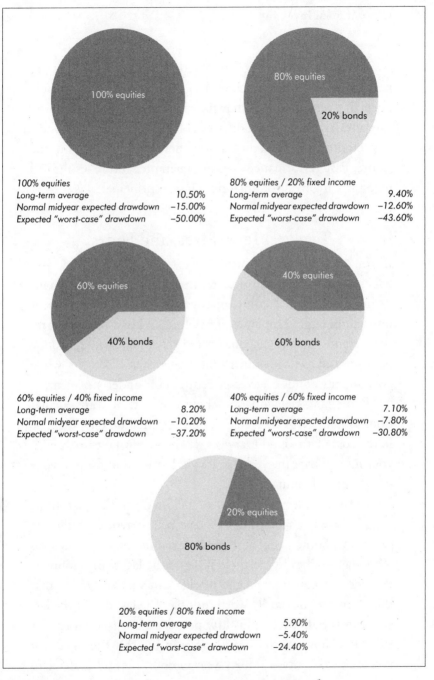

100% equities
Long-term average	10.50%
Normal midyear expected drawdown	–15.00%
Expected "worst-case" drawdown	–50.00%

80% equities / 20% fixed income
Long-term average	9.40%
Normal midyear expected drawdown	–12.60%
Expected "worst-case" drawdown	–43.60%

60% equities / 40% fixed income
Long-term average	8.20%
Normal midyear expected drawdown	–10.20%
Expected "worst-case" drawdown	–37.20%

40% equities / 60% fixed income
Long-term average	7.10%
Normal midyear expected drawdown	–7.80%
Expected "worst-case" drawdown	–30.80%

20% equities / 80% fixed income
Long-term average	5.90%
Normal midyear expected drawdown	–5.40%
Expected "worst-case" drawdown	–24.40%

Figure 6. Average returns on asset-allocation options[*]

---

[*] Data source: Fidelity, iShares, NYU Stern School of Business.

In figure 6, asset-allocation return figures reflect (1) expected average long-term returns, (2) expected (completely normal) average annual drawdown, and (3) expected worst-case annual loss — given different blends of stocks and bonds. Expectations are based on history. There are no facts about the future. Past performance does not guarantee future results. All investing involves risk, including loss of principal.

Twelves, Tens, Sixes, and Fours

If you look at any twenty- or thirty-plus-year period, you will see consistent historical returns for certain types of investments. For small companies, you'll see about a 12 percent return. For large companies, it will be closer to a 10 percent return. Bonds have much smaller returns, of course. Corporate bonds see an average return a bit higher than 6 percent, while government bonds on average return a bit under 5 percent.

Remember that inflation should be part of your calculations as well. With an average 3 percent inflation rate, that rise in the cost of goods and services will be in constant battle with your returns over the years, so it's vital to account for it in your investment planning.

Most people are mentally anchored in the last three months, the last six months, the last year, maybe even the last two years. Some people are hardly even looking at trends for a full day — they're mostly looking at the last thirty minutes. But the last half hour in the market can vary so greatly that the variations are hardly worth noting. The last day or the last year can vary between plus fifty points and negative forty. It's ridiculous how much noise there is in the short term! But if you look at twenty- to thirty-year periods, they all coalesce to a close range around these long-term averages. The longer you look at your investments within each of these categories, the

more likely you are to converge on the 12, 10, 6, and 5 percent returns, always mitigated by that 3 percent inflation rate.
Those numbers serve as the long-term anchors for returns in
these various categories.

When building a portfolio, you should be thinking about
having more of those twelves and tens and fewer of those
sixes and fives. It's important to not base investment decisions
around the short-term volatility that's happened in the last
year, month, or hour. Yes, you'll have to brace yourself for
some turbulence — but don't be scared by it. If you're anchored in the right amount of equities, you'll be seeing those
twelves and tens, and those are returns well worth the ups and
downs.

As we've discussed, the reality is that life is getting more
expensive; cash doesn't keep up with inflation, bonds barely
do, and equities do it wonderfully. In fact, one of the best tools
for overcoming inflation is your equity dividends — which
will multiply at two to three times the rate of inflation. The
more of your portfolio you commit to owning equities, the
higher the probability you will outperform the need for future
income and the higher the probability your income will rise
to meet your rising cost of living (and then begin to outpace
it). In the simplest terms, the calibration between stocks and
bonds in your portfolio reflects a choice between meeting the
real need to have your income rise to meet your rising cost of
living and meeting the emotional need to reduce your portfolio's short-term volatility. More of the one means less of the
other. Ask yourself which is more important to you.

Idiot-Proof Investing

In planning anyone's portfolio, including my own, I like
to establish what I call the 5 percent rule, aka idiot-proof

investing. I have no doubt in my mind that with any portfolio blend, even one that is conservatively balanced — say,
40 percent fixed income — I can achieve a long-term 5 percent return. So, with any asset allocation, I can use 5 percent
as my absolute baseline for returns. With this idiot-proof rule
in mind, you can skip a few steps in the early planning stages
of your portfolio. Determine your need, determine how much
you will be able to save, then plug in 5 percent as your return on investment. If you can meet your financial goals using
5 percent returns (which you're likely to beat), then you're in
great shape in terms of your savings, lifestyle, retirement goals,
and so forth.

Time Is of the Essence

When he was twelve, my son Eli started working at the local
pool. He would sweep, clean, take the garbage out, uncover
the pool, and perform other basic tasks. By the time he was
fifteen, he was sick of that job and found one at a local deli
instead. One year we were doing our family's taxes and a friend
of mine jabbed us playfully, saying something like "Wait, why
do you claim Eli's taxes? It's not even worth paying the fee, just
keep it under the table and let him keep all his money."

Well, we wanted to pay his taxes. The reason behind that
decision was simple for us: if Eli filed his taxes — even when
his income barely surpassed $200 one summer — we were
able to put that $200 into a Roth IRA for him. Same for his
sister, Annie, when she was old enough to work. And because
Eli and Annie grew up with a financial adviser for a dad who
insisted on a rule of thirds for everything the kids made —
one-third into savings, one-third to giving, and one-third for
spending — my kids both have Roth IRAs already growing
for their futures. Initially my wife and I didn't add any extra

money to them, but the kids still understood that if they start the saving and investing habit now, they would be *way* better off when they're older. This year we decided to add to (and max out) the kids' Roths. I believe parents should do this, to the extent possible. As I write this, Eli is only eighteen and Annie is fifteen. Time is most certainly on their side.

Sometimes I think about that savings account I opened with fifty dollars back when I was a kid. If I had continued adding to that account for the last forty years, I'd have had a pretty chunky savings by now.

That said, I have a lot of clients who come to me at thirty-five, forty, forty-five years old who haven't even set up an IRA yet. Maybe they have a 401K through work, but they're not contributing as much as they could be. That's not ideal, but you have to start where you are. If your retirement accounts have already been cooking for twenty years by the time you're thirty-five, you're in great shape. But if not, there's no time like the present. You might have to make some trade-offs — like working longer, saving more, and spending less — but it's far better to realize that now than five or ten years from now, or when you're looking at your final paycheck and wondering how you're going to pay the bills for the last third of your life. Sounds grim, I know.

When Time and Expectations Don't Align

I had a client I'll call Nick who didn't start his investing plan until he was thirty-five. Originally, Nick's goal was to buy a house "ASAP," retire by sixty, and support his son through college. Red flag number one was the vagueness of his plan. ASAP is not an easily attainable goal because there's no specific timeline attached to it. Nick's entire plan was in his head. In fact, it wasn't a plan at all. It was a set of wishes. They were great wishes, but to turn them into achievable goals we had to make a plan so they could come to fruition.

For Nick to retire by sixty, he only had twenty-five working years left in which he could add to his portfolio. But it was a starting point. Once we understood Nick's goals, we were able to see how much he'd realistically need to set aside over that twenty-five-year span. Considering Nick's rising income, his rising cost of living, his savings account, his son's college tuition, and how much longer Nick would need income beyond retirement, we're talking quite a bit of money.

Next, we looked at how Nick could allocate his portfolio. The idea of allocating too much of his assets to equities made Nick nervous, so we determined that he was on the moderate side of the risk chart. Nick felt most comfortable with the idea of a 30/70 blend of equities to bonds. So we looked at what the return on a 30/70 blend would likely be over the next twenty-five years. Using Vanguard's historical risk/return data from a hundred-plus-year period as an example,* I showed Nick that a 30/70 blend would produce an average return of about 6.7 percent. Taking into account inflation, that would mean an average, long-term real return of about 3.7 percent.

That return of 3.7 percent over twenty-five years would not bring in enough money for Nick to meet all his goals. I challenged Nick to shift his standing on the risk scale to see what would happen if we went just a little more aggressive. We looked at what would happen if we flipped his portfolio to an asset allocation of 70 percent equities and 30 percent bonds. This would provide Nick with a long-term return closer to 8.9 percent (or 5.9 percent after accounting for inflation) over the next twenty-five years. As we always say in the business,

---

* "Portfolio Allocations: Historical Index Risk/Return (1926–2019)," Vanguard, n.d., advisors.vanguard.com.

past returns are no guarantee of future results — but they're a helpful reminder of what we typically see over extended periods of time.

Going for a 70/30 asset allocation was going to involve a major mindset shift on Nick's part. He would need to remind himself that over time the markets *will* go down — and thus, his accounts *will* dip — but if all of history is an indicator, markets will come back up again, as will Nick's accounts. It's a matter of sitting patiently and nonreactively during the ebbs and flows.

Here's the thing: based on our calculations,* if Nick were to achieve all the above goals — retirement age, paying for his son's tuition, continuing his spending and savings habits — he would need to see a return on his investment accounts of about 15 percent. Even if he were to shift his asset allocation to 100 percent equities, there is just no way that type of return would be possible. Even the most aggressive portfolio is rarely going to see much more than a 10 percent return over its lifetime. Nick had to make some trade-offs and mindset shifts.

The one thing Nick knew he did *not* want to give up was paying for his son's college tuition. So that would remain a fixed expense. Nick had to consider what other sacrifices he could make to meet his long-term financial goals. The first trade-off Nick was willing to make was in his spending and savings habits. There were several areas in Nick's life where he could cut down on spending (eating out, travel, those all-too-familiar impulse buys). The second trade-off was his retirement age. Nick decided he'd be willing to work another five years and retire at sixty-five, giving him that many more years to contribute to his retirement accounts. Another option would be for him to make

---

* If you're curious about how to make these calculations, check out the *Mindful Money* book or the course on my website, mindful.money.

more money, but that was only a *possibility*, not a *definite* — so we planned around what we knew.

The third change Nick made was in his asset allocation. After plenty of coaching and promises that his financial advisers would help him resist the urge to jump ship anytime the markets dipped, Nick decided to shift his asset allocation to a more aggressive blend of 80 percent stocks and 20 percent bonds. This type of asset allocation would bring Nick's portfolio returns up from about 6.7 percent to more like 9.4 percent over the next thirty years, which would make a sizable difference in his earnings. Again, these numbers are based on historical average returns for an 80/20 asset allocation and are never a guarantee — but if we use history as our guide (and it's the only one we have), these estimates should be pretty darn close.

As an aside, note that interest rates on bonds have been steadily declining over the last forty years or so. This means that although bonds have historically given us certain returns in the past, they offer *non-repeatable* returns in the future. If rates continue their decline, we'll see an even lower return on bonds in the future. Equities, however, have historically done the opposite. Over the last forty, sixty, eighty, one hundred years and counting, the return on equities has continued its steady incline and there's no reason to believe that such growth will not continue.[*]

But back to Nick. Yes, there have been times when Nick has had to grip the wheel of his metaphorical ship and not

---

[*]   Remember: investing in equities means you're investing in business. As the cost of living continues to go up, the cost of business goes up right along with it. Markets measure the voluntary transactions between billions of people for goods and services that make their own and their families' lives better.

bail when the markets dipped and his accounts declined. But he's been able to weather those storms and wait for his accounts to come back up again. Which so far, a decade into the process, they have. Now Nick is sitting more peacefully knowing that both his son's future and his own are realistically accounted for.

Aside from the right asset allocation, time is one of the most important factors influencing your investment plan. The more time you can give your investments, the more that interest can compound and the more growth you'll see. But the old cliché exists for a reason, which is to say that it's always better late than never.

Stimulus, Response

American existential psychologist Rollo May wrote in *The Courage to Create*, "Human freedom involves our capacity to pause between the stimulus and response and, in that pause, to choose the one response toward which we wish to throw our weight. The capacity to create ourselves, based upon this freedom, is inseparable from consciousness or self-awareness."* Throughout his work, May stressed the importance of acknowledging the central role of decision-making in the human experience — and how a pause can lead to better choices.

Our most valuable emotional asset in investment planning is our ability to *not* react when the market goes down. To the extent that we practice this, we have control over whether we will fail. If you knew there was a simple rule you could follow that would drastically improve your investment outcomes, you would follow it, right? And if you *knew* that the number

---

* Rollo May, *The Courage to Create* (New York: W. W. Norton, 1975), 100.

one cause of investment failure is panicking and following an emotional response — that is, reacting rather than pausing and then doing nothing — why would you not practice that skill? The smartest investors are not the ones who listen to the latest news and make frequent buy-sell decisions. They're the ones who are nonreactive to the noise and practice the art of the pause. If you can put this into practice, you can create a portfolio that has more equities (or, like mine, 100 percent equities) and sit mindfully when things go down, knowing that your long-term returns will be worth the nonreactivity. Just wait patiently for the markets to come back up again, which they have always done in the past.

You've probably seen those online ads that say things like "Learn this ONE trick to reducing belly fat!" Or "Learn ONE trick for building a seven-figure online business!" Those are usually touting useless products or services involving a lot more money and steps than the ads imply. In this case, however, there really is one trick that works, doesn't cost anything, and is incredibly effortless once you get the hang of it. Do nothing. That's it. That's the secret to the long-term success of your portfolio. The right asset allocation, broad diversification, and regular rebalancing of your portfolio are all vital ingredients in your investment recipe. And the key to the success of that portfolio is the art of doing nothing when markets go down.

Remember Andy, the guy from chapter 5 who kept firing his financial advisers, changing his asset allocation, and losing money? His biggest mistake was his lack of an investment philosophy guided by the belief that the markets will always recover. Every time the markets went down, rather than weathering the storm and waiting until the clouds had cleared, Andy changed course. He did that repeatedly and wound up making little progress on his path to financial freedom. If Andy had practiced the art of the mindful pause, chosen nonreaction, and stayed the course, his accounts would have recovered, and he'd be sitting pretty right about now. The only way to enjoy the market's permanent advance is to sit quietly and nonreactively through its temporary declines.

You *have* to first develop your trust that the markets will recover and then build that belief into your investment philosophy. Developing that mindset is a matter of patience and discipline, not of intelligence or guesswork. You just believe the markets will recover and learn to ignore the impulse to get out when they drop.

The markets have *always* recovered and there is no evidence to suggest this will change in the future. Yet again and again we're sucked into the worry that they will *not* recover because our panic and the naysayers are telling us that this time it's different and everyone should get out of the market. In fact, another rise will come, another crash will come, and overall the markets will continue to climb.

Just as important as it is to believe that the markets will recover is acknowledging that markets *will* go sideways. It'll get scary, but if your belief that the markets will recover is solid and you can just be patient, you will have an income stream in retirement that outpaces your needs.

That's the goal. Sounds wonderful, right? If we had all the tools to achieve that, why wouldn't we make it happen? As long as you commit a greater percentage of your portfolio to equities and a smaller percentage to bonds, you will create that rising income stream. And you'll keep it, as long as you can stay nonreactive to the market's vagaries. Be as sure of this as you can *before* committing to your asset allocation. If your belief is strong and you can stomach more volatility without panicking, why would you choose to *not* have higher outcomes? Why would I create a fixed income in a rising-cost world when I could have a rising income in a rising-cost world?

A Mindset, a Driver, and the Beginning of a Plan

There are three variables that need to match up when creating your financial plan: how much you can save, how much your returns are, and how much you're expecting to spend. You must choose a driver to take you on your investment journey. If you choose risk tolerance as your primary driver, it means you're going to limit how much you can spend, which will demand that you save more. It's simple math. If you can't accept greater volatility as a trade-off, your lower risk tolerance means lower returns. And that may not be the best choice. Would you rather consistently reduce spending or increase the risk in your portfolio to see a higher return on your investments over the long run? One involves mindfully reducing your spending and one involves mindfully doing nothing.

Since you will have to deal with these variables, really *look* at all three.

Say you've made your financial plan and see that you'll have enough. In your plan, maybe you've determined that you only need a 4 percent return. Maybe you have a strategy in place, you've saved enough, and you can meet all your future expectations and all your future income needs with a conservative portfolio. Maybe you're risk averse, that's all the risk you want to take, and you're not interested in trying to earn more. That's fine.

The problem is that most people never plan. They never know what they really need. Instead, they go on feelings, such as "I don't like the feeling of volatility so I'm going to be conservative." What that means is they end up not having enough for retirement. Or they do the opposite and hope for enormous returns in the latest fad investments. Since they never thought about it, they're not making the trade-offs that would *enable* them to stick with conservative portfolios, primarily saving more to offset the lower returns. And if they're not saving more, they'll never have enough.

Fundamentally, this fear of volatility is why we have a retirement-income crisis today. That, and the fact that none of us saves enough. Well, you can't have it both ways. You need a rising income stream. That is a fact. To get that rising income stream, either you must save a lot more or your portfolio has to perform better. If you can manage to do both, then you're in good shape! And if you can save more, choose to invest in equities, *and* start when you're really young? Oh my gosh, you're in *great* shape.

The vital piece is the planning, so that you have a realistic idea of what you'll need for retirement and make any necessary trade-offs. If you just sit back with a conservative portfolio without saving enough, you will not have an income that rises. That's just math.

MINDFUL INVESTING ACTIVITY

Here's where it all starts to come together — which is to say, where we take everything you've learned in the book so far and begin to map out the next steps in your personal financial journey. It's a lot, so revisit the relevant exercises and resources, including the planning calculators and other guidance on my website at mindful.money/resources and, for more detail on big-picture financial planning, the companion to this book, *Mindful Money*. Copy these questions into your notebook and answer each as accurately and honestly as possible:

- What are your long-term goals, particularly what you'll need for a comfortable retirement?
- How much do you have saved already?

- How much can you realistically continue to save and add to your portfolio to achieve your financial goals — including when and how you'd like to retire?

To check whether you're on the right track, revisit the asset-allocation chart in chapter 9.

CHAPTER 11

Diversification
(Not Prognostication)

You can never plan the future by the past.
— EDMUND BURKE

Diversification is a deal we make with heaven. We accept that we will never make a killing, in exchange for the priceless blessing of never getting killed. Not taking on the risk of buying individual stocks means accepting that we won't see massive gains — but we won't see massive losses either. And as we've said before, no one can know which stocks will do well and which will tank, or when.

The idea is to own it all. Own every sector, manufacturers of every product, and providers of every service. Own companies in the United States, Europe, Asia, Africa, and South America. From small-cap companies to large-cap companies, own them all. By broadly diversifying, we're admitting that we don't know who is going to win the battle, and we understand that we don't *have* to know to be successful. There are plenty of examples of how this plays out. Let's start with computers.

Computers: Argument #1
for the Total Market Portfolio

If you were looking for a computer in the late '90s and early 2000s there were plenty of manufacturers to choose from, notably Apple, HP, Gateway, and Dell. Over time, the thing that had more and more people going with Dell was its ease of use. Dell had what it called its Direct Model, in which you could buy a computer directly from the company, have it customized to your needs, and speak with in-house customer support staff as needed.

In the late '90s, Dell's stock value rose steadily from less than a buck per share in 1995 to ten dollars per share by 1997. By 1998, shares of Dell were teetering between thirty and forty dollars per share. A lot of people knew that computer companies were hot stocks by the late '90s; it was just hard to know which company to go with.

If you happened to have bought Dell stocks back when their shares cost pennies, you could have made a fortune! Then again, if you had waited until the company was clearly on the rise and bought in the year 2000, when shares were about forty dollars apiece, and held on to them in hopes of even bigger gains, you would have lost a massive amount when they dropped to thirteen dollars in the 2010s. A lot of people made money, a lot of people lost money, and a lot of formerly enthusiastic investors were suddenly stressed as hell about the technology sector.

Conversely, if you owned a little piece of *every* computer manufacturer, you wouldn't care who won the dominant market position. If you own Apple and Dell and Acer and all the other manufacturers, you won't care how they do relative to one another; the only thing you'll need to be concerned about is that people keep buying computers (a pretty good bet!).

Because as long as people are buying computers, that money is going to the bottom line of at least one of the companies you own.

Here's the thing: by buying little parts of every computer manufacturer that exists, you give up the potential upside of guessing the right answer to the question "Which is the winner here?" But you don't have to worry about the huge potential downside of getting it wrong. The beautiful simplicity of this practice is that you don't have to know if it'll be Apple or Dell or Acer that does well for your portfolio to be successful.

A secondary benefit is that the top companies change hands many times throughout their lifetime. For example, in 1997 when Apple almost went under, Microsoft — at the time its main competitor in computer software — bailed the company out with a massive investment. Who would have thought? The point is that it's never obvious who will be the winner in any industry. Owning them all means you will own the eventual winner, which comes with a lot of advantages:

- You don't have to keep thinking about it all the time.
- You don't have to stay on top of the news.
- You don't have to worry when the business you thought was going to win gets passed by another one.
- You don't have to change horses halfway through the race.
- By committing to diversified ownership, you are betting on the consumers, not the companies. That's a good bet.

Computers aren't going anywhere. If you're able to keep more conservative assumptions in your planning — that is, maintaining the belief that the computer industry will continue its growth — then you don't have to be right about who will win or lose. And you know what? Pretty much all the research says that most people guess wrong.* If even the people with great access to information and the ability to talk to CEOs and suppliers can't outperform the market, then what hope do those of us with no access have?

You might be thinking, "How am I supposed to own them all?" The answer is simple: you buy broadly diversified funds or ETFs. We call this owning the total market portfolio, meaning a little sliver of every type of company that exists, weighted to reflect each sector's presence in the economy (like the Vanguard Total Stock Market Index Fund we talked about in chapter 9). There are plenty of different index and mutual funds out there. You can buy industry-specific funds like tech funds or green energy funds, or more broadly diversified funds, like the Russell 3000 (again, see chapter 9). I like to think even bigger with the Wilshire 5000, which has even more slivers of top US companies (five thousand, naturally). The point is to own it all. Own every sector of every size in every place, and accept that in doing so, you'll never make a killing but you'll never get killed.

Tires, Banks, and Argument #2 for the Total Market Portfolio

Bridgestone, Goodride, Michelin, Goodyear, Hankook, Firestone, Dunlop, Falken, Chaoyang — all these manufacturers make tires, with reputations ranging from "Safest on the

---

*   Jeff Sommer, "Mutual Funds That Consistently Beat the Market? Not One of 2,132," *New York Times*, December 2, 2022; "SPIVA Data," SPIVA: S&P Dow Jones Indices, n.d., https://spglobal.com/spdji /en/research-insights/spiva/; "Don't Bother Trying to Pick Stocks" Dimensional.com, June 13, 2019.

road!" to "Avoid these killers at all costs." Over the decades, we've seen dozens of tire manufacturers come and go. Some of these companies have been acquired by larger manufacturers and some of them are no longer in production, but the fact is this: people are buying tires and, for the foreseeable future, people will continue to buy tires. You don't need to bother guessing which tire companies will do well and which will go out of business. Own them all.

Another example of the "own it all" philosophy? Banks. The financial crisis of 2007 and 2008 was the biggest market downturn since the Great Depression. No one predicted that the savings and loan Washington Mutual or the investment bank Bear Stearns would collapse as a result (both were subsequently bought by JPMorgan Chase, a choice CEO Jamie Dimon soon regretted).

If you received a letter in the mail saying that your bank went under, you wouldn't just stop using banks altogether, right? You would just move your accounts to a different bank. Millions of Americans received such notices. The result? The biggest banks got bigger. Without getting into any societal commentary here, the key takeaway is we cannot reliably predict which banks will be successful, but we *do* know that banks as a whole are not going anywhere. The first proto-banks appeared around 2000 BCE, so it's a solid bet that banks will continue to exist and generate profits. By owning every bank, you don't need to worry about *which* bank will last through the decades (or centuries, or even millennia!).

The question is, do you buy shares of each individual category — tires, computers, banks, and everything else out there? Not quite. The act of choosing any individual sector is itself a decision about what's going to be successful. By buying a total market portfolio, you're buying every type of asset available in the entire investment world. A Russell 3000–based portfolio is not divided equally between its three thousand company holdings; it is weighted according to each company's presence in the market. Maybe 5.1 percent of the fund is in Apple, 1 percent is in JPMorgan Chase, 0.00008 percent is in Goodyear, and so on (these are estimated examples, not exact numbers).

Bottom line: you want to buy broad categories that will include every sector. As the cost of living increases — defined as the price of these goods and services we're investing in — the worth of these companies is going to naturally increase over time. If you own a little piece of everything, your portfolio earnings will increase along with that cost of living and eventually surpass it. If you stay broadly diversified, you have to accept that you'll never be the top performer, and that's okay. You just need to perform steadily, not better than everyone else. In a world defined by the desire for *more*, we only really need to seek *enough*.

Global Markets

In 1980, Apple opened a corporate office in Cork, Ireland. In 1985, Microsoft followed suit and opened a corporate office in Dublin. In 2003, Google opened an office in Dublin as well. The list goes on and, as you might have guessed, it's not just the Guinness they're enjoying.

In a twenty-plus-year effort to attract American and other international companies to set up shop in Ireland, the country has maintained an incredibly low corporate tax rate. As is true for most industries, the number one goal for companies looking for desk space in Ireland is to produce higher profits for their shareholders. A lower corporate tax rate means exactly that. So when Microsoft establishes an office in Dublin and some of its intellectual property ownership is in Ireland, a huge piece of the value of the products they produce, even if they're assembled or compiled in the United States, is attributable to that intellectual property in Ireland. The way markets function globally — even if we're talking about the same American companies with operations outside their home country — is that different nations have different tax structures, which translates into different returns on the shares of those companies regardless of where you live.

In an initiative spearheaded by US secretary of the treasury Janet Yellen in 2021, over 130 countries — Ireland included — agreed to set a minimum global corporate tax rate of 15 percent, which will have a huge effect on this tax loophole.[*] This minimum still compares well to the current US corporate tax rate of 21 percent.[†] The bottom line is whether it's due to tax structures, new trends, international laws, or global crises, markets respond differently in the United States from the way they do in Ireland, France, Bermuda, or Singapore.

Another factor is the cost of labor. In France, it is incredibly difficult to lay off employees because of the nation's worker-centric policies. In the United States, by comparison, you can lay off employees anytime you want. Sure, there are expenses involved in the process, but they are far less than they would be in France and many other European countries. The opposite is true for China.

There, it is much cheaper to hire employees. Chinese companies are not required to offer many benefits, so most do not allow bathroom breaks, their buildings might not have

---

[*]   Implementation of this agreement remains to be seen, as of early 2023.

[†]   The 21 percent rate is the result of the Tax Cuts and Jobs Act of 2017, which dropped the top US corporate tax rate from 35 percent while eliminating tax-reduction loopholes (such as foreign-sourced income deductions).

air-conditioning in triple-digit weather, employees might be paid very low wages, and they can be fired at any time for any reason. Not having to pay for employee benefits is a huge incentive for companies to set up manufacturing facilities. Opening and maintaining offices in places like China is often seen as a win-win: Chinese people are given job opportunities they wouldn't have otherwise, and the company sees lower expenses and higher profits, which means more money to shareholders. Whether this is sufficient or ethical is far too complex to get into here — there are a range of similarly valid ways of looking at the labor situation in China, and a lot of reading you can do to better understand the trade-offs. *

Of course, there are added expenses for manufacturing in places like China, like taxes and international shipping costs. Plus, any global company must account for supply chain issues, employment issues, tax issues, transportation issues, access to materials, determining the best location to manufacture components, how to recruit and hire people with higher education levels in emerging nations... the list goes on. The important thing for investors to understand is this: being broadly diversified gives you access to, *and* subjects you to, changing environments all the time. The goal is to expose your portfolio to a wide range of markets.

---

* Every investor must choose whether (and the extent to which) they wish to reflect their values in their investment decisions. We touch on the concept of ESG (environmental, social, and governance) investing a bit below, but it is beyond the scope of this book to elucidate the depth of this topic. In my opinion, ESG investing within reason will have a negligible effect on your outcomes and is therefore a good idea. Too strict an adherence to ESG investing has a potential cost borne by the investor (in terms of lost potential performance), but in such cases the investor is often happy to trade away some performance to adhere to their ethics more closely.

Emerging Markets and the Final Frontier

When we talk about global diversification, we're primarily referring to three categories: the United States, developed countries outside the United States, and emerging markets. There is also a fourth category known as "frontier markets," which are much higher risk and typically not recommended for most investors.

Emerging markets are not terribly far off from developed markets. As Investopedia puts it, an emerging market is defined as "a developing nation that is becoming more engaged with global markets as it grows."* Emerging markets can be summed up as low-income but rapidly industrializing countries like Mexico, Russia, China, and Brazil. These economies are typically growing very quickly, which means they potentially offer big gains for foreign investors. Of course, their economies being less stable means that investing there poses a higher risk and is typically only recommended for people who can stomach the inevitable declines and afford any potential losses.

Even less stable and riskier are the frontier markets. These are countries whose economies are less advanced and are much less stable than those of emerging markets, but still more stable than the least developed countries. Frontier markets include countries like Kenya, Bangladesh, Kuwait, and Bahrain. These nations have developed market economies with maybe a few companies to invest in, but they are still very unstable. Frontier markets usually have poor liquidity and are likely to see big fluctuations in currency values — let alone the real concern that their governments might be subject to a coup

---

* Investopedia Team, "Emerging Market Economy Definition: Examples and How They Work," Investopedia.com, updated May 11, 2022.

tomorrow. The unsteadiness of these markets is what makes them risky. There is the potential to lose a whole lot of money. But there is also the potential for monumental gains.

A great example of a frontier market success story is Nigeria. Specifically, Nollywood. Back in the early '90s, an electronics salesman named Kenneth Nnebue ordered a large shipment of blank VHS tapes. In a country where many homes did not have televisions, let alone VCRs, Nnebue soon learned that no one wanted to buy his tapes. A creative entrepreneur, Nnebue solved his blank-tape problem by writing a script, finding a producer and director, and filming his movie *Living in Bondage*, the story of a businessman who turns to witchcraft to become successful. Nnebue had the film copied onto his excessive blank-tape inventory and sold it straight to the public.

These days we think of direct-to-video movies as commercially unsuccessful. In the case of *Living in Bondage*? Quite the opposite. The film helped spark the multibillion-dollar Nigerian film industry known as Nollywood. Investors who saw the potential in this industry early on would see big returns in the coming years — not by any means an everyday story for a frontier market. The *Harvard Business Review* used the Nollywood boom as an example of the "market-creating innovation" theory. In the January 2019 article "Cracking Frontier Markets," authors Clayton M. Christensen, Efosa Ojomo, and Karen Dillon argue that what's missing from the conversation around frontier-market investment is the power of innovation. In the case of the Nigerian film industry, there was a severe lack of access to — or supply of — Nigerian films. Once entrepreneurs who knew the market found a creative way to fill that gap, the target audience responded enthusiastically, and market profits responded too.

As Christensen, Ojomo, and Dillon say, "Nollywood is among scores of entities that have realized enormous growth by creating entirely new markets where they might least be expected." But most frontier markets don't behave like this. There are countless stories of new companies that started as great ideas but did not succeed. Frontier markets offer enormous opportunity, but at massive, unpredictable risk. For this reason, most of us shouldn't add them to our portfolios unless we have not only the time and expertise to keep up with the latest advancements in these nations but also the resources to accept loss when it may come — which in this case, is more likely than in any other market.

Bolts and Burgers:
Why Company Size Matters

To illustrate this point, imagine a small (fictional) Chicago-based manufacturer we'll call Illinois Bolts. This imaginary company specializes in making one type of bolt and is successful. Since the company is so small and has only one plant, its success is subject to the geography, employment space, tax rates, intelligence, and innovation available in the Chicago metropolitan area. It has access to capital from a great local bank. What it *doesn't* have access to is the global capital markets that big, established manufacturing companies do.

By comparison, let's look at the very real General Electric. GE manufactures everything from dishwashers to aircraft engines and sources its materials from all over the planet. It's got engineers and designers from all over the world bringing their unique perspectives and expertise to the table. With all these resources, GE is creating new products all the time. It gets to source capital and materials from anywhere it likes; the company is not tied to a local environment like Illinois Bolts is. But by the same token, GE is *already* everywhere.

Because GE is a global company, it doesn't have the opportunity to create new material-sourcing relationships; it already has access to all of them. GE can't reduce its cost infrastructure in the same way that a small company like Illinois Bolts can. Since Illinois Bolts has a higher cost structure, it still has the flexibility to grow, to source new materials, and to reduce costs. GE's costs, on the other hand, are already reduced about as far as they can be. Simply put, GE is established and doesn't have a whole lot more room to grow, while Illinois Bolts has plenty of growth capacity should it move in that direction. That's why diversification across company size is an important consideration in your portfolio: differently sized companies offer different growth opportunities, different options for creating new products, and different returns on investment.

Another great example? Burgers. Take the California-born burger chain In-N-Out. In 1948, the first In-N-Out was founded in the Los Angeles suburb of Baldwin Park. Founders Harry and Esther Snyder wanted to create a burger joint that would serve quality food quickly, hence the name. The chain slowly spread throughout California and beyond, with some big milestones reached in the 2000s. In 2008, it opened its first restaurant in Utah; in 2011, its first in Texas; in 2015, it opened its three hundredth location and its first in Oregon. By the end of 2021, there were 358 In-N-Out locations and counting.*

Now take McDonald's. Also a burger joint, also established in California in the 1940s, also focused on speedy delivery and simple burgers — but with a very different growth

---

* "History," In-N-Out.com, n.d.

story. As you may have seen in the 2016 movie *The Founder*, entrepreneur Ray Kroc discovered Mac and Dick McDonald's small burger joint in San Bernardino, California, in 1954. He was impressed by their simple menu and "Speedee Service System." Long story short, Kroc helped create the McDonald's franchise. A mere four years later, McDonald's had sold its millionth burger. By 1967 McDonald's had gone international with its first restaurant in Canada, as well as one in the US territory of Puerto Rico. In 1990 Moscow got its first McDonald's; in 2003 the "I'm lovin' it" campaign was a big hit; and in 2020 McDonald's opened its first net-zero, carbon-neutral restaurant at Disney World in Florida. The company now has over thirty-seven thousand locations worldwide with some 1.7 million employees and is worth about $47 billion.[*]

That is a lot of burgers.

As an investor, diversification in company size is important. You want to invest in both bigger and smaller companies. You want the Illinois Bolts and the GEs, the In-N-Outs and the McDonald's. Why? Because large and small companies have quite different return profiles and opportunities to improve. McDonald's is already all over the world. There is a McDonald's in Prague and a McDonald's in Sydney, in dozens and dozens of locations worldwide, from Hong Kong to Manila to Guantanamo Bay. The company is so huge that its opportunities for growth are much different than those for In-N-Out, which is still expanding gradually across the US West and Southwest. The global expansion factor is important. Sometimes, due to geopolitical factors, one currency will be favored over another for investment; sometimes big companies will be favored because they'll have access to global capital markets

---

[*]   "McDonald's History," corporate.mcdonalds.com, n.d.

that small companies will not. You want your portfolio to have benefit from both the growth potential of small companies and the stability of larger companies.

Public and Private Sector

I believe that 99 percent of people should stick to investing in public markets, but it is worth a brief discussion here of the diversification that can happen between public and private markets. As companies wait longer and longer to go public, they're able to reserve more of their potential upside in the company for insiders (like venture capitalists and private equity firms). This means that there is a reason to think that over extended periods, a small exposure to private markets would be desirable. However, there are enormous risks to investing in private markets; even more than with publicly traded stocks, it's always difficult to know which company might succeed and which will not. Additionally, with any private investment, you are almost always working with people who know a lot more than you, which means that staying on top of your investment may mean managing a lot more information than you are equipped to handle.

A Final Argument for the
Total Market Portfolio

When the United States had a big meltdown in 2008, most banks stopped lending to smaller companies, a trend we still see in 2023. Banks are always much more likely to lend to bigger companies, which means that bigger companies have resources that are not available to their smaller peers. Just as investing in both big and small companies changes your opportunities and your risks, so does investing in global and emerging markets. The key is to have broad access to changing environments, which evens out your performance over the long term.

There are thousands of companies. A lot of people say, "Well, if I just buy the S&P 500, I'm diversified." My response to that is yes, sort of. The S&P 500 is a collection of very large and very *domestic* companies. There are close to five thousand publicly traded companies in the United States alone. If you were to go with the Wilshire 5000 and invest in every publicly traded company in the nation, there are bound to be opportunities there that you wouldn't see otherwise.

Within these thousands of companies, there are inevitably going to be risks as well. Some of those companies may go under and some may just not do as well, but by balancing opportunities and risks you get to engage in the full gamut of opportunities. Investing in all these companies is also a way to protect yourself, because even if companies you've invested in *do* go under, they'll have less effect on your overall portfolio so you don't have to worry too much.

One of the main goals of my personal investment strategy is not having to spend too much time and energy thinking about my investments. Time is the only finite resource, as they say. So why waste yours carefully selecting companies that you think *might* do well, and then spending even more time monitoring their performance? I have a friend who used to spend fifteen to twenty minutes every day checking her stocks and then throughout the day read every notification her investment app sent. It didn't seem like much time until one day she saw somewhere that if you read for twenty minutes a day, you can read ten to twenty books a year (depending on the books and your reading speed). That was ten to twenty more books than she had been reading. The point is that my friend realized that she could be spending her time in much more healthy and productive ways than by checking her portfolio daily. Curious about how someone like my friend could recalibrate her investment strategy and set up her investments on as close as you can get to autopilot? Read on.

MINDFUL INVESTING ACTIVITY

This is an easy one!

Remember everything we've discussed so far about why diversification is essential to achieving *predictable, stable* long-term results. The simplest action items here are the following:

- **Invest in everything:** Own every size company in every sector in (almost) every place, and accept that in doing so you'll never make a killing but you'll never get killed.
- **Consider the total market options:** Choose a highly diversified fund or ETF (or set of funds and ETFs) that includes tiny slivers of thousands of companies based in the United States, developed markets, and emerging markets.
- **Don't get cute with it:** Only venture into frontier markets, private markets, or popular new investments once you've got a portfolio that will meet your minimum goals and you've both the money to risk and the time and interest to stay on top of those sectors. For most investors, this won't be worth the time, effort, and anxiety.

CHAPTER 12

Do Nothing, Nothing, Nothing ... Then Rebalance

Better one safe way than a hundred
on which you cannot reckon.

— AESOP

A lot of people ask me, "What is *the* most important rule in investing?" My answer to this question won't change, regardless of the person's circumstance, age, or location. The most important thing you can do as an investor is not, as is commonly assumed, selecting the right companies to invest in at just the right time. It's not regularly checking your portfolio. And it's certainly not regularly *shifting* your portfolio. I trust this doesn't come as too much of a shock at this point in the book, but the single most important thing you can do as an investor is to be in the market at all. Simple, right? If you're already in the market, then you're already getting somewhere, and somewhere is better than nowhere.

What's even more simple is that once you've made your plan-appropriate asset allocation and created a broadly diversified portfolio, the next most important thing you can do is ... nothing. Or next to nothing.

Nonaction and Simplification

Every kid has had the experience of being picked on — whether by a sibling or a classmate — to the point of reaction, whether that means hurling insults right back or slugging the other kid in the face. I used to come home from school with sob stories justifying any reason I might have gotten in trouble at school, all of them boiling down to "They started it!" It's a common story — one kid says a mean thing, the other kid reacts, the whole thing escalates, and then both kids get in trouble. Whenever that happened to me at school, my mother would say something like "Well, Jonathan, next time don't respond." As if it were that easy! While that act of doing nothing would have saved me a lot of grief, sometimes doing nothing is one of the hardest things to accomplish. Not responding involves mindfulness; it requires that you acknowledge what's going on, pause between the stimulus and your response, and then choose to respond thoughtfully rather than emotionally.

In chapter 3 I introduced the Taoist concept of *wu-wei*, which essentially means "no action" or "doing by not doing." *Wu-wei* holds that one of the most powerful actions we can take is no action at all. We've already addressed this concept to some degree, but as we transition into talking about account maintenance I find it helpful to reiterate.* If we own the entire market and are able to patiently follow the practice of *wu-wei*, we *will* see growth in our accounts over time.

That said, the only nonrenewable resource is time, right? The goal is to organize our accounts in such a way that they are

---

* Also recall the Rollo May quote from chapter 10: "Human freedom involves our capacity to pause between the stimulus and response and, in that pause, to choose the one response toward which we wish to throw our weight. The capacity to create ourselves, based upon this freedom, is inseparable from consciousness or self-awareness."

functioning on as close to autopilot as we can get them so that we can spend more time on the things we enjoy, the things that bring meaning to our lives. We can also choose to spend that extra time earning more money, which is an action over which we *can* have control (as opposed to playing the markets, which we *can't* control).

When I say as *close* to autopilot as possible, this means there are some regular acts of maintenance that are important to keep up with. We've just reviewed two of the three key practices to follow for a successful portfolio: plan-appropriate asset allocation and diversification. The third practice, rebalancing, should involve only a few hours of your time each year.

From Volatility Comes Rebalancing

In 2021, J.P. Morgan produced a report indicating that in the forty-two-year period from 1980 through 2022, despite an average intra-year drop of 14 percent, annual market returns were positive in thirty-two of those forty-three years. The average annual return over that period was 9.4 percent. So even when we saw dips in the market over those decades, most years were positive — so much so that the cumulative positives outweigh the cumulative negatives by an average of 9.4 percent per year. See figure 7 on the next page.

For example, in February 2012 markets went down by 10 percent, but the year still ended with a growth of 13 percent. In 2019 there was a period of the year where markets were down 7 percent, and yet the year finished up by almost 30 percent. Perhaps the best example is 2020, the first year of the pandemic, where markets dropped 34 percent in a matter of thirty-three days, then recovered all of that loss and added an additional 16 percent before year's end. The point is that these down cycles happen, but they have no bearing on how

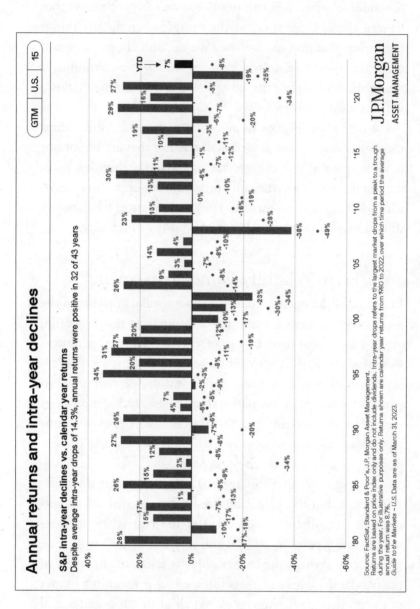

Figure 7. Annual returns and intra-year declines. (Courtesy of J.P. Morgan Asset Management.)

any particular year turns out — and they certainly don't define a twenty- or thirty-year period. Maintaining a long-term investment mindset is key to cultivating a successful portfolio. After deciding which asset allocation we need to follow to reach our long-term investment goals, it's important to understand that peaks and troughs *will* throw our portfolios off from the original asset-allocation percentages we established. But since we're expecting those fluctuations, we can plan our response ahead of time by committing to regularly rebalancing our portfolio among and within asset classes. In other words, we rebalance not only the overall mix of equities and fixed income, but also the individual equity or fixed income investments in our account.

Let's say you've got a moderate, 60/40 blend of equities to bonds, and over the course of a year the stock market is on the rise. Say that in the span of that year your portfolio migrated from a 60/40 blend to a 72/28 blend. This type of shift is inevitable. In order to maintain the long-term allocations you strategically set up, you've got to rebalance your portfolio, which in this case means selling some (12 percent, to be precise) of those equities and buying more bonds to get your portfolio back to the 60/40 allocation that you determined will meet your goals. See figure 8 on the next page.

Billionaire and investor extraordinaire Warren Buffett is known for focusing on accumulation opportunities and future growth. He says his favorite holding time for a stock is "forever." He subscribes to a school of investment that says, "Buy and hold." There is another school that says, "Buy, then look for good deals and trade." But *my* favorite school says, "Buy, buy, buy, and hold. Then occasionally rebalance." Keep consistently adding more shares to your portfolio every month then rebalance once or twice a year. That is the secret to successful accumulation versus speculation.

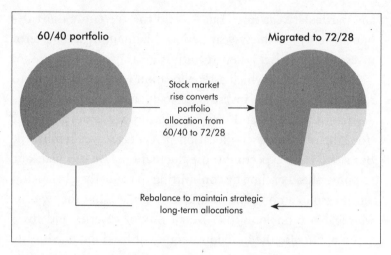

Figure 8. The rebalancing process: sell equities; buy bonds

Trigger-Point or Calendar Rebalancing?

As we know, markets are volatile: they *will* go up and they *will* go down, and you can't reliably predict when or to what degree. It's futile to spend any time worrying about market volatility, because it's just something that happens. But what you *can* do is mindfully choose how and when to rebalance your accounts when the markets knock them off course.

There are two ways you can rebalance: by calendar year, which means choosing one to two regular, recurring times each year to rebalance, or by trigger point, which means re-acting to a specific change in the market and rebalancing your accounts accordingly. A lot of people ask me which rebalancing practice is better; really, there's not a huge difference in terms of the returns you'll see. Some like going with calendar rebalancing because it's the simplest to plan for. Say you select New Year's Day as your rebalancing date. Great! You just put "January 1: Rebalance!" on your calendar and you don't need to think about your accounts at all for the rest of the year. There is nothing more to it than that. For most people, calendar rebalancing is a great way to go.

If you go with trigger-point rebalancing, you must determine what your trigger will be; whenever your portfolio hits the threshold you set, you rebalance. Trigger-point rebalancing involves paying a little more attention to your portfolio than calendar rebalancing, so some people do a hybrid model, which is how we operate at my firm. Using the above example of the client with a portfolio model of 60/40 and a trigger point of 20 percent, should their equities reach 72 percent of their portfolio (twelve being 20 percent of sixty), we'd sell some of their equities and buy more bonds, so their portfolio is rebalanced back to an asset allocation of 60/40.

Let's take the market's response to Covid-19 as an example. Within a few weeks, markets dropped dramatically. By the end of March 2020, they were down by about 30 percent. At that point, our firm decided to rebalance because we believed the markets would recover — which they did, and much more rapidly than we'd expected. A month after the Covid-19 market response, the markets had already bottomed out and were on their way back up.

That means a drop in stock prices brought down the value of the equity component of our clients' portfolios. Therefore, we sold some of their fixed income assets and used the funds from those sales to buy more of the now low-priced equities while their prices were still low.* This is nothing more than putting into practice the old maxim "Buy low, sell high," which is the natural consequence of either form of rebalancing.

Let's say that at the beginning of 2020 your portfolio was

---

* I say "still" because we do this knowing that the prices won't stay low forever. And when they do come back up, we'll have made a profit.

allocated to an 80/20 blend of equities to fixed income. When the value of the companies you were invested in dropped by 30 percent that March, your portfolio value would have shifted pretty dramatically, right? At that moment, the value of your equities would no longer be 80 percent of your portfolio, but more like 74 percent. If you had $80,000 in stock and $20,000 in bonds, you would now have $56,000 in stock and $20,000 in bonds (assuming for the example your bonds didn't move much), and your new total allocation would be 74/26. In this case you would sell 6 percent of your bond portfolio and buy stocks with the proceeds.

Any time you rebalance, you'll have to sell some of whatever is higher (in this example, your fixed income) and buy more of the asset that is currently down (here, your existing equities) while the prices are low (in other words, once again, buy low, sell high). If you'd rebalanced in March 2020, you would have seen a big bump in the overall value of your portfolio in the weeks after the market rebounded.

The standard rebalance trigger is when there's a 10 or 20 percent change. Anything much more than that would occur far less frequently. For example, if you set your trigger point as high as 50 percent, that means that you'd only rebalance when the markets dropped by 50 percent or more. Well, this is a turn of events that only happens once every decade or so. If a 50 percent market decline were your trigger point, you'd be missing a lot of opportunities for buying low and selling high throughout those years when the market had smaller dips and spikes and you *didn't* rebalance.*

---

*   For a more in-depth look at rebalancing statistics, I suggest checking out Michael Kitces's post "Finding the Optimal Rebalancing Frequency: Time Horizons vs. Tolerance Bands," *Nerd's Eye View* (blog), May 4, 2016, kitces.com.

The benefit — and risk — of a trigger-point rebalance is that you get overweighted to something that is in favor *right now*. However, the winds often shift more quickly than you can rebalance. In March 2020, by the time we rebalanced about a month after the trigger-point drop, the markets were already on their way back up (a recovery speed that is almost unheard of, by the way). Conversely, with a calendar-based plan, you'd have been rebalancing every year on the same date regardless, which means you'd have seen much slower and steadier progress. Simply put, trigger-point rebalancing is more involved and active than calendar rebalancing, without much additional benefit.

There are two key benefits of the calendar rebalance. The first is that it maintains your risk profile in a better way than trigger-point rebalancing does. If the way you set up your portfolios is based on expected return versus expected risk — and if you already pushed your equity exposure to the limit when you built your portfolio — you don't necessarily want to let the markets push it further. Why? Because then we just set ourselves up for fear and panicking, and as we know, panicking often leads to rash decisions — like selling when markets drop. The second, huge benefit to the calendar rebalance is that you only have to look at your portfolio once a year. It's less involved and saves more of your precious time.

Plan-appropriate asset allocation, broad diversification, and rebalancing are what I call the trifecta of successful investment practices. This allows for peace of mind; you don't have to worry about what will happen next because you already own everything, and you don't have to worry about timing because you have a disciplined rebalancing process that takes into account the market's natural ebb and flow. This simple practice frees you from trying to outperform the markets.

Instead, you're capturing the expected returns over long periods of time. By contrast, investors who *do* attempt to outperform the market end up with lower-than-expected returns because they tend to buy and sell at the wrong times for the wrong reasons. In other words, capturing expected returns may be the best you can hope for.

I like to refer to "Buy low, sell high" as "Buy the losers and sell the winners." Regular rebalancing is nothing more complicated than selling some of the current winners so you can buy more of the current losers. Given this, how do we know how much and how often to contribute to our portfolios?

Dollar-Cost Averaging:
A Simple Way to Outperform the Index

If compound interest is the eighth wonder of the world, dollar-cost averaging is the ninth. Dollar-cost averaging is an investment strategy wherein you allocate a set amount of money at regular, short intervals to investments that are a little more volatile (which is to say, stocks and stock mutual funds). The best example of this is a 401K in which you deposit a set amount every month, regardless of share prices. This means that you always invest the same *amount* on your investment accounts each month, but the number of shares you buy depends on what price they're at. This allows for you to reduce your per-cost basis. How?

A specific investment is volatile, meaning it goes up, it goes down, then it goes up and down again. For example, let's say that you consistently invest one hundred dollars per month into an index fund. If the share price in March is twenty dollars, you'll buy five shares. In April, the share price goes up to twenty-five dollars per share; your hundred dollars now buys you four shares. Maybe a few years ago shares were ten dollars so your hundred dollars bought you ten shares.

Regardless of share price, you're always putting one hundred dollars per month toward that account and buying more or fewer shares depending on what that hundred will buy you that month. Over, say, thirty years, this means you are always trying to reduce your cost basis. Thus you have an *average* cost per share to use in the long term when looking at your total ownership and profits.

The key here is that you're making a regular *monthly* contribution rather than, say, saving that hundred dollars a month and then investing the whole $1,200 in a lump sum at the end of the year. With twelve entry points throughout the year at varying share prices rather than the one annual one, you will on average get a lower cost basis. What this means is that as the account goes up in value, you get bigger gains.

Dollar-cost averaging is a wonderful tool that allows you to outperform your own index and your own managers — simply because you're buying more shares when they're cheaper and fewer when they're more expensive. The other major upside is that you never have to worry about trying to buy at just the right moment. Having a set monthly investment amount allows you to sit mindfully and do nothing aside from letting your investments grow. You don't have to pay attention to the stock prices of the day because you're contributing the same amount each month, with a dollar-cost average that outperforms the index.

Once again, we see that investing is simple stuff; the hard part is learning how to *not* pay attention to the financial news of the day, the month, the year, and to just think about the long term. It's not sexy, but it *will* pay off.

Automated Investing: When to Turn It On, When to Turn It Off

These days we can automate just about everything. You can set your thermostat to turn on and off at specific times or temperatures each day of the week; you can have medications for yourself or your pets delivered each month before you run out; you can set all your bills on autopay. So why not set your investments on auto as well?

Automation is what I like to call mindful mindlessness. You set up your regularly recurring contributions each month then let dollar-cost averaging and compound interest work their magic. Another important tool within the automation realm is to reinvest your dividends each month. This feature is available on any online investment account (just be sure to turn it on) or you can set it up with a financial adviser.

Many clients have asked me if they should stop reinvesting dividends in order to give themselves more liquidity when it comes time to make their quarterly tax payments (more on that below). In this case, I explain that failing to reinvest your dividends will result in greater cash drag, which means holding a portion of your portfolio in cash rather than reinvesting it. Sitting on cash in a portfolio earns you returns that are too low to offset inflation. If your investment funds are producing, say, a 10 percent return and you automatically reinvest those dividends each month, they will also earn you 10 percent, right? Sure, you can choose not to reinvest your dividends and keep your cash waiting for you when the taxman calls, but this decision will result in lower performance.

Yes, you will be paying more taxes (because you'll be making more money), but your return will increase at a higher rate than your taxes, so I see no reason to *ever* turn your dividends into cash. If you end up *having* to sell some of those dividends later to pay your taxes, you'll still be better off than if you had kept that money in cash earning you nothing or waiting to invest until you felt more comfortable doing so.

This brings me to another issue: once you've taken your dividends in cash you're no longer in the realm of automation, and you *must* decide how and when to reinvest that money — and we humans are naturally inclined to want to invest at the wrong times. An important thing to remember about the psychology of investing is that our brains want to invest when things look good, when we should be investing when things look bad. To paraphrase Baron Nathan Mayer Rothschild, a nineteenth-century English-German financier, the time to buy is when there's blood in the streets.

Returning to the great rebalance of 2020: stock prices went way down, so we sold our fixed income assets to buy more of those "loser" stocks. When those stock prices went right back up again, we saw a high return on our investments. Sell the winners, buy the losers.

Bottom line: if you set up automatic reinvestments, your mind won't be able to get in its own way. You won't have to make any decisions; you will let automation work its magic and you'll see incrementally higher returns as a result. The one exception to this rule is when you're actively pulling from your investment accounts in retirement because the accounts you pull from every year will depend on your current tax bracket.

An Aside on Peakiness
(Kids, Don't Try This at Home)

There was *one* time in my twenty-five-plus-year career when I felt the market was looking pretty peaky, meaning really overvalued. This was in late 2019 when the stock market was booming. I thought I should do something about this.

As you may have gathered by now, this is the wrong thought nine times out of ten. But it was hard to escape the siren song urging me to act. I knew I should *not* change my strategy because of what the media was telling me, but it was hard to resist. Before acting, I tried the following exercise. I asked myself what I would do if I was right and the market really *was* peaky. One strategy I thought of was to slow down my investments temporarily by putting a hold on my dividend reinvesting. I recognized that I would get reinvested when the market felt less peaky, but until it was I wanted more control of those reinvestments.

The decision to stop reinvesting is not something that we should take lightly. To take such an action is to ignore all the research saying it can't be done successfully.* If things really are getting peaky, of course you *can* take a break from reinvesting dividends for a while. But it's important to pause and acknowledge your thought process and your feelings first. When you hear that siren song, you won't be alone. Others will have the same feeling and the media will be fueling the flames. This is why the siren song works — *if* you let it. The key is to know beforehand that the song is coming. Automation is like Odysseus tying himself to the mast to prevent him from giving in at the precise moment he knows he shouldn't.

Don't Forget the Taxman

During Leona Helmsley's 1989 court trial, one of her housekeeping staff testified that she had heard Helmsley say, "We

---

* "Does Market Timing Work?," Schwab.com, July 15, 2021; "Timing the Market Is Futile," Morningstar.com, April 3, 2020; "What Happens When You Fail at Market Timing," Dimensional.com, July 29, 2022; "Timing Isn't Everything," Dimensional.com, July 1, 2019.

don't pay taxes. Only the little people pay taxes."* By trial's end, the billionaire real estate investor and hotel operator, famously dubbed "The Queen of Mean," was sentenced to eighteen months in federal prison for tax evasion.

Little people, big people, and in-between people all must pay taxes. There is no safe way to escape the taxman unless you want to wind up like Helmsley, or at least mired in back taxes and headaches. But there are some things that we can do to minimize our taxes and avoid double taxation on our hard-earned money. At this point, we've covered the three primary strategies for building a successful portfolio: asset allocation, diversification, and rebalancing. The fourth leg of the table is tax management.

First, take advantage of things like 401Ks, IRAs, SEP plans, SIMPLE 401Ks, and SIMPLE IRAs. These types of accounts allow you to put money away for retirement on a tax-free basis, for a couple of reasons. Say we have a client who's retiring. This client doesn't have a pension and their Social Security income will be about $30,000 a year. Federal guidelines state that any individual with an adjusted gross income of less than $82,000 per year does not have to pay any capital gains tax† and can take advantage of a much lower income tax rate. So how would this client take advantage of that?

If the client has an IRA, a Roth IRA, and a taxable portfolio, they can choose from which of those they will draw for their income. This allows them to manage their income level to keep it below that $82,000 number. This allows the client to minimize the tax drag (i.e., loss of income due to taxes) on

---

*   "Maid Testifies Helmsley Denied Paying Taxes," *New York Times*, July 12, 1989.

†   Of course, the capital gains taxation rules are subject to change. What's here describes the situation as I write this in early 2023.

their investments, which is one of the *best* methods of making their money last longer in retirement.*

Capital gains are not taxed until you recognize them. If you have investments that spin off an income stream, they are the ones to put in an IRA, a 401K, or something else that's tax managed, so you don't have to pay tax on the income. If you have a taxable portfolio, you can build a large bank of unrealized gains you can use to take from in the future, and you won't have to pay any capital gains tax on them in the interim.

Socially Responsible Investing

Among all the different index funds, mutual funds, and ETFs available, there are an increasing number of socially responsible funds to choose from. These funds are composed of companies that are committed to making a positive social or sustainable impact. However, how each of us defines "socially responsible" is going to be different. If, for example, you're a humanist in the Bay Area, you might not want to invest in anything related to weapons manufacturing; if you're Catholic, you may want to support organizations that oppose abortion; if reducing the impacts of global warming is important to you, you might want to support companies that have made a commitment to reducing their carbon footprint.

There are lots of ways companies can choose to commit to their brand of social responsibility. As I write this in 2023, sustainability is one of the biggest factors people look for when selecting socially responsible investments. Companies all over the world show their sustainability efforts differently. For instance, Microsoft has a whole department dedicated to

---

* I always recommend speaking with a tax adviser when setting up these accounts and determining how much money to pull each month.

sustainability and is pushing efforts to become carbon negative by 2030. In 2019 Amazon created the Climate Pledge, which is a commitment to reach net-zero carbon by 2040. There are lots of funds and ETFs to choose from and lots of causes to support with your investments.

A couple of things here. First, each company's definition of "sustainable" varies. The term itself is still so loosely defined that it's hard to set specified parameters for what constitutes a successful effort. Thus it's no surprise that there has been a lot of concern about accountability. The SEC warns that many misleading claims are made around the term "socially responsible," which is not particularly well defined. These types of funds are still fairly new in the investment world, so if putting your investments toward companies whose social responsibility is important to you, it might be worth doing a little digging to understand what their efforts really mean.

The second thing to keep in mind is, well, money. Is investing in socially responsible funds something that will increase your investment returns? Not necessarily. Whether you invest in socially responsible funds or those who claim no social responsibility, there is no real difference in terms of what your returns will be. The real importance is how broadly diversified you are across every size, every geography, and every type of business. Whether it's tire companies, burgers, computers, or pharmaceuticals, the crucial thing is to appropriately allocate your assets among broadly diversified funds.

Pursuing social responsibility is something that's becoming increasingly important to a lot of investors. Keep in mind that it is unpredictable how utilizing the different definitions of social responsibility will affect your performance in the short term, but it probably won't affect your performance in the long term by much. Being ethical in all areas of your life (including your investments, however you define ethical investing) makes a ton of sense. We can all benefit from acknowledging that we are living interdependent lives and that the earth is part of that interdependent ecosystem. This is an important pursuit. And, if you keep it reasonable — avoid the idea that something is "bad" because it is profit seeking — your long-term financial success will neither be aided nor harmed by your investing with your ethics in mind, so long as you asset-allocate appropriately, stay broadly diversified, and rebalance regularly.

MINDFUL INVESTING ACTIVITY

You guessed it, it's time to review and reiterate the key themes in this chapter (which we've also been exploring and explaining throughout the prior chapters).

In your notebook, write down this list, in nice big letters, and revisit it as needed if you're feeling anxious or eager to start messing with the plan:

1.   MAKE MY PLAN-APPROPRIATE ASSET ALLOCATION.

2.   CREATE A BROADLY DIVERSIFIED PORTFOLIO.

3.   DO (ALMOST) NOTHING.

4.   REBALANCE REGULARLY.

CHAPTER 13

Angel Investing

A wise man will make more opportunities than he finds.
— FRANCIS BACON

In my first book, *Mindful Money*, we explored how to identify your personal values and, once you do, how to translate
them into your work and the rest of your life. One key exercise in that book involves developing your unique purpose
statement, which might be something like "I write stories to
connect people," or "I teach peace," or "I educate people about
mindful money practices." The goal is to ask ourselves what
would make our lives feel well lived.

The entire financial structure of your life should be based
on how *you* define success. That might be finding a job that
you love so much it doesn't even feel like work, or working
hard during the day so that you can do all the fun things you
want in your free time. The goal is to have control over your
own time, since that's the only finite resource, right?

Part of what I love about angel investing is that I get to
help other people fulfill *their* dreams and be able to do what
they want with their time. That's not to say that every project that receives angel investing is someone's life dream; some

people move on to create many worthy endeavors over their lifetime. But part of what brings me joy as an angel investor is seeking out those projects that I believe in, with *founders* I believe in. Often, people think of angel investing as not so much investing in a company but investing in the person or persons *behind* a company. In fact, many angel investors are friends, family members, or individuals otherwise personally connected to the company founder in some way who want to support them for personal reasons.

Angel investors (also known as seed investors, private investors, or angel funders) are ready to invest money before most investors are. Angels are there at the very start of the company's concept and usually make a one-time investment, or they might contribute several times throughout the beginning stages of the company. And when I say "company," I'm not necessarily talking about the next Facebook. Many of the projects that receive angel funding are started by entrepreneurs creating small local businesses or online services. Maybe someone is opening a restaurant, a little bookstore, or a coffee shop and needs some start-up capital for rent and supplies. That person might ask friends and family to invest money in their business so they can get started. If the business does well, their friends and family will receive their investment back with interest. If it doesn't, they might lose everything.

Many projects will not succeed, which is part of what makes angel investing incredibly risky and not something I'd recommend for anyone who doesn't have the money to spare. That being said, I do participate in several angel investments because I know the incentives, I know the market, and I know the person behind the project. And hey, maybe their project will still fail for whatever reason — maybe it was too early to market, maybe it was too late, maybe the competition was better. But not only do I understand the incentives and risks behind each individual angel investment I make, but I understand business, so I am able to project more easily what might happen than someone who doesn't. I like to think of angel investing as another layer of diversification with the potential for rich rewards, but with *much* higher risks than most types of investments.

As interesting as angel investments are, they are typically not worth their considerable risk. Angel investing should be thought of as something you can try after all your other bases are covered: you've got your emergency fund saved up, your debts paid off, and your investment accounts set to auto-contribute their monthly maximums. If you have a little extra money to play with, angel investing can be an incredible way to support projects and people you care about.

Gaming Angel

Aside from my drive to support friends and family, I commit to angel investing because I *love* entrepreneurship. I have so much respect for people who want to build something from nothing, who remain flexible and push forward when setbacks come, and who work hard to try something new. That, to me, deserves a gold medal. It's fun for me to be involved in someone else's creation and to be able to contribute however I can.

One of my favorite angel investments is one I've written about elsewhere, and that is the story of my good friend Gary (whom I introduced in chapter 3). I've known Gary since my twenties. For years, Gary was my Dungeon Master (or DM, as we say in the *Dungeons & Dragons* world). He wrote incredible, intricate stories and was just this insanely intelligent and creative guy whom I enjoyed hanging out with.

About eighteen years ago a bunch of us were playing *D&D*

and Gary shared that the company where he worked as an IT manager looked like it was about to go under — which it did. A few months later, Gary was the IT manager at a different company, but he just wasn't happy. Sure, he was making good money, but what were his days like? Pretty exhausting. So one night in the middle of a game he told us he was thinking about starting a game store.

Everyone at the table agreed wholeheartedly that this was a great idea. What better person to run a game store than a huge gamer who sleeps and breathes this stuff? Gary would build these elaborate worlds, and he'd spend money on the stuff we needed to make them immersive and believable. He was incredible at the game, and there was no doubt in my mind that if Gary opened a game store, he would put his heart and soul into making it succeed. This wasn't just another job. This was Gary's passion.

Initially, Gary thought he might buy an existing game store. I accompanied him to a couple different stores, where he interviewed the owners and gathered some information. But Gary had a vision. He wanted to start a store all his own. And he did it with a plan. Rather than start out in a primo location with the perfect space, Gary rented a storefront that was a little off the beaten path but with enough foot traffic and parking to help bring in the right customers. By doing so, he was able to save money on rent and use those extra funds to build up an incredible inventory.

I didn't become an angel investor for Gary's store because I thought the return on my investment would float me into an early retirement. I invested in Gary's company because I believed in Gary. I know him, I know gaming, and I understand business. The fun part for me (besides getting to come in and peruse some of the best inventory in the Bay Area) was watching the business take shape and getting to advise along the way. I love being engaged in that part; it brings me joy to share my expertise and to see someone's great idea become a great business. And guess what? Gary's store *did* become a great business. Sure, it had some rocky patches in the beginning, but now it's thriving. Gary gets to do what he loves with his time, and he no longer has to push through that familiar feeling of "Ugh, I have to go to work today." Now it's "I *get* to go to work today," coupled with "I get to work whenever I want."

These days, Gary has the freedom to make his own choices; he's his own boss rather than having to work when and where someone else tells him to. He's an incredible example of someone investing in themselves and their own happiness, and that's an investment I like to be a part of.

Choosing the Right Investments

Some people ask me what green or red flags to look for when agreeing to be an angel investor. I say, if you're going to embark on the angel investing journey, you've got to do your research. Angel investing makes up a small percentage of my portfolio. Again, I don't do it because I think I'll rake in the dough, but rather because it's fun. I've made some investments in bigger projects that didn't work out, and I lost that money. Conversely, I've made more modest investments in smaller companies that ended up doing well.

How did Gary's game store become such a success? Perhaps there was some luck involved; perhaps it was perfect timing. Yes, when I chose to invest in Gary's company, I believed in him, but there was no reason to think he would be more successful than anybody else. The sad truth is that many start-ups, with all different kinds of founders across all different industries, do not succeed. Gary's store has been around for eighteen years now. During that time, about a dozen others have tried to compete with him and none of them has made it. Gary talks about this other guy who is a big gamer but a terrible business owner, as evidenced by the fact that he's already opened and closed four stores. Establishing a successful business involves passion and a mind for business, along with good timing and a little luck. And often it's incredibly hard to predict which companies will last and which will fold.

If you're thinking about investing *all* your money in angel investments, I'd counsel you not to. Instead, think about setting aside no more than 5 to 10 percent of your overall portfolio for these types of endeavors.

Smaller Ways to Be an Angel Investor

With Gary's business, the investment process wasn't too formal. We did create a management agreement, but we didn't get attorneys involved because, like the other guys who invested money up front, we were good friends with Gary, and we'd see him Saturday night at our next *D&D* game anyway. That is to say, we weren't worried about the legitimacy of Gary's business or the value of his word — just whether the spooky caverns he created for our game were going to be filled with nasty goblins!

With larger undertakings, it's more complicated. Many angel investors make over $200,000 per year and can invest anywhere from $10,000 to $100,000 in a start-up without too much worry about potential losses. These investors will meet with the founder(s) as well as a team of advisers, attorneys, and experts to draft up an agreement around what kinds of returns investors will see and when. Again, this is an area where doing your research is important, and it's paramount to set the expectation that *this might not work*.

There are, of course, much smaller ways to invest in new companies, such as Kickstarter or GoFundMe. These crowd-funding sites allow you to support projects ranging from new restaurants to tutoring services, nonprofits to documentaries, card games to new kinds of toothbrushes. Contributors can invest anywhere from a few dollars to thousands, and their investment returns will vary accordingly. For many projects, the return on investment is being able to participate in the project early — participating in the documentary or getting one of the first sustainable toothbrushes off the production line.

Patreon is another option to investigate. This crowdfunding site supports creatives by allowing people to pay a monthly subscription fee to artists. The artists, in return, offer specialized, subscriber-only content. Sites like these allow entrepreneurs to reach a larger audience than if they were to simply send out an email to friends and family asking for support. Of course, these sites take a fee, and in cases where a specific investing goal isn't reached the money is returned to investors and the project gets nothing. All of this is to say, there are smaller, less risky ways to invest in the power of entrepreneurship if that's something that brings you joy but you don't have the funds to risk on angel investing.

Blueprint to Storefront

In the last few years, and especially since Covid-19, people are finding new and innovative ways to work. Just type "side hustle" into a browser and you'll see an enormous number of suggestions for gig work. You'll also see lots of small service companies starting up. People are realizing that the nine-to-five lifestyle, working at a job that they don't love, is not something they *have* to do. Many are starting their own businesses. As the term *side* hustle implies, these gigs often overlap with a conventional job in the beginning. Lots of folks are working that extra hustle for ten or twenty hours a week until that *side* shifts to *main*.

That is something I have incredible respect for. It's not easy to look at what you value in life, to understand what it is you're good at and want to do with your time, then to take steps to *do* that thing. So as an angel investor, I keep an eye out for these folks and support their journeys if I can.

For me, angel investing is not something I want to spend a whole lot of time and energy on. Yes, I love participating in planning meetings and giving my advice. I love watching a dreamscape become a blueprint, an inspiration become a storefront. But I didn't start looking at angel investments until I was financially ready (meaning that my portfolio was in good shape and I had a little extra wiggle room). These types of high-risk investments account for less than 10 percent of my portfolio; the rest of my money is invested just how we've described in the previous chapters. In fact, I'd like to share exactly how I invest. Read on.

MINDFUL INVESTING ACTIVITY

Angel investing should always be the thing you do for fun, to help your community, or to support an idea you really believe in — but only once you have implemented an investment plan to provide for your financial future. Remember, it is highly unlikely that you'll get rich with this kind of investment, and you might even lose everything you put in if the idea doesn't pan out. Here are some questions to ask yourself before you take the plunge:

- Are you passionate about the business idea?
- Are you knowledgeable enough about it to make smart decisions?
- Do you have a good head for entrepreneurship and business?
- Does the person or entity you're considering investing in also have a good head for those things?
- Can you make this investment for fun and *potential* profit without endangering your long-term financial goals?

CHAPTER 14

How I Invest

Our lives are not totally random.
We make commitments,
we cause things to happen.

— WENDY WASSERSTEIN

Remember that Antoine de Saint-Exupéry quote that we touched on in the first chapter, "A goal without a plan is just a wish"? As you've probably gathered by this point in the book, I'm a big planner. I've had many clients over the years come to me with big ideas for the future, like those who say they want to have their house paid off by the time they're fifty-five, retire by sixty-five, and support their kids through college and their parents in old age, all the while taking fun annual vacations, driving nice cars, and eating out all the time. Those are wonderful, achievable goals — but financial goals don't just happen to us, they happen *because* of us.

With any big goal, the only way to get there — aside from wild, unreliable luck — is to plan. One of the foundational steps in my personal investment practices is to understand where I want to go and how to get there, then to take it one step at a time until I've arrived. My own planning is guided by the philosophy that to even make a goal in the first place, we must set aside our limiting beliefs.

Guiding Principles, Limiting Beliefs

One of the biggest lessons my parents taught me was to *always* save. My mom stressed the importance of a "rainy-day fund" and saving, saving, saving. She made sure we understood that anytime you make money, you should put a little bit away. She never referred to this practice as "pay yourself first," but that's what it was.

When I was a kid, I thought that $100 was a lot of money. But as my dad liked to say, "Big numbers are just little numbers with more zeros." He meant that it's all relative. Once you've saved $100, you realize it wasn't so hard. In fact, it was very attainable. Then you save $1,000 and the same thing happens. Then $10,000.

Usually, as your earnings grow, both your savings and your lifestyle grow along with them. When you're younger, $100 *is* a lot of money. Then when you get a bit older, $100 is a little bit of money and $10,000 is a lot. Then you graduate college and get a job and $10,000 is reachable but $100,000 seems impossible. Then $100,000 is attained and $1,000,000 seems a stretch. But then as you get older you realize that a million isn't *that* much money. It's more than most have but it's not enough money to retire on in most cases.

At every point in this journey, we looked at something and thought that getting there would be impossible. What my dad was trying to tell me is that there is a natural increase as we age. It is normal to earn, save, invest, and grow more and more. Don't be shocked or afraid. Don't worry about it or overthink it. "More zeros" is a normal part of the process.

When I was in my early twenties and had just graduated

from college, I thought that making $100,000 or more was something I could never do. It was just such a huge number. With big goals and big numbers, many of us think this way, but saying "I'll never be able to" or "I don't think it's possible for me" is a way of limiting ourselves.

In her 1992 book *A Return to Love: Reflections on the Principles of "A Course of Miracles,"* Marianne Williamson wrote, "Our deepest fear is not that we are inadequate. Our deepest fear is that we are powerful beyond measure. It is our light, not our darkness, that most frightens us. We ask ourselves, who am I to be brilliant, gorgeous, talented, fabulous? Actually, who are you *not* to be?" This is an extraordinary concept! With any big idea — whether it's increasing your income by a zero or starting your dream business — I say why *not* you?

Many writers, philosophers, and motivational speakers have touched on the same concept. In his 1978 book *Illusions: The Adventures of a Reluctant Messiah*, for instance, Richard Bach wrote, "Argue for your limitations and, sure enough, they're yours."

The point is if you insist that you can't do much, you're going to be right. In terms of your earnings, if you think of higher income goals as "just more zeros," it helps quiet that limiting belief. And if you think of yourself as worthy and capable of even setting those goals in the first place — and then planning to achieve them — you're going to be right about that too.

Step by Step

In almost any industry, if you want to grow a larger revenue, you must either offer larger-ticket items or scale up production of smaller ones. If you're a painting contractor, you don't just stick with lower-paid gigs painting the house next door.

You either expand your business to include commercial buildings, or you scale up and do more of those smaller jobs. There isn't really any other way to do it. This concept applies to retail, to financial advising, to writing, to marketing services, to anything: you find a way to offer bigger-ticket items, or you scale up the number of smaller-ticket ones you can perform.

Of course, you must provide more value to charge higher prices — but you can do that. It's just a matter of learning a new way of doing something, improving your skill set, and increasing your offer. It'll be hard work, which a lot of people are afraid of, but you can do it. There is no reason to give up before you even try, saying "I can't do this" or "I could, if *only*..." Everyone has some sort of limitation or obstacle, it's just a matter of figuring out how to work around it.

There is no reason to think that you can't scale, make more, or do the important or interesting thing you really want. People do it every day, so why not you? Remember Richard Bach: "Argue for your limitations and, sure enough, they're yours."

When I first moved from Dean Witter to Paine Webber, I told my manager that my goal was to manage $100 million. I thought that was an enormous amount and that it'd make me feel successful and excited to get there. My manager looked up from his coffee and said, "I have no doubt in my mind that you'll get there." It seemed crazy to me that he said this so casually, making it seem such an attainable goal.

And then when I *did* hit that goal, it really *didn't* feel so impressive anymore. I looked back and thought, *Okay, that was doable. Here's how I did it. Now I know how, so let's do it again but better.* The goal moved to managing $200 million, then $300 million. What I learned in that process was that when I was looking forward, my goals seemed huge and difficult to achieve. It was hard to imagine who I'd be once I hit that benchmark.

As with any kind of planning, the key is to *set* your goals, figure out the path you need to reach them, and then pursue that path. Once you get there, you set another goal, and with enough time and effort you'll get there too. It's a matter of pushing aside those limiting beliefs and putting a stop to the limiting talk. Belief in yourself is key to your success.

Past Returns, Future Success

I first started in the finance industry during the dot-com era. I was a glorified salesman, and my side gig was to trade options. I would buy ten thousand calls on a stock, meaning the right to buy that many shares at a particular price before a particular date. Sometimes I made money, sometimes I lost money. The only constant was stress.

There was one time when I bought about twenty thousand calls of a company called Juniper Networks. A few days later, the price went down, so I doubled down and bought twenty thousand more calls, hoping that would save me. The price kept moving against me, so I doubled down yet again. I ended up owning one hundred thousand calls of this stock. I don't remember how much money I had tied up in the trade, but I do recall spending a lot of time just staring at the screen, totally stressed out, willing the price of Juniper Networks to go back up.

One day the stock moved positively a little bit and I got back to "almost even." I immediately liquidated my position because I couldn't handle the stress anymore. As it turned out, the stock kept going up without me. If I had stayed in, I would have made something like $200,000. But frankly it wasn't worth the stress, including all the time I spent thinking about that stock and checking in on it. I could have been putting my time and energy into much more productive things.

Sure, there were times when I made a lot of money for myself or my clients. But I think of the phrase "past returns are no guarantee of future success." Just because a certain trade worked at one point does not mean it will work again. In fact, chances are it will not.

There were plenty of times during my Wall Street years when I made similar investments, but Juniper was one of my biggest options trades and it was my last. Occasionally, when the idea of trading seems appealing again, I remind myself of Juniper and the stress, the potential loss, all the time I put into looking at my screen, and the energy I spent thinking about it. It was not worth it to me. I still believe strongly in the power and necessity of equities, but these days I have a much different relationship with them. I keep things simple, simple, simple.

My Asset-Allocation and Investment Philosophies

I am an equity fanatic. An equity zealot. A true believer. What does that look like for my accounts? I favor 100 percent equities for my investment portfolio. I do not invest in bonds because the return rate is not high enough, and because I believe in the markets over the long term. I can stomach the zigs and zags over the years because I have faith that any downward turn will come right back up again. I know that not everyone can stomach that, and that's perfectly fine. I am also aware that the more funds you have invested, and the larger your income stream, the easier it is to invest in all equities because you don't *need* to rely on your investments in the same way. You have more wiggle room, so to speak.

I have been in the financial industry for more than two decades. It is by trying everything and seeing how it really works that I have landed on three core investment philosophies:

1. Establish an emergency fund first.
2. Put 90 percent of your investable capital in diversified global equities (with a plan-appropriate bond ballast).
3. Put the remaining 10 percent of investments into something fun (however you might define that).

My funds are invested in just the way I've talked about throughout this book, and I did that in the order outlined above. My portfolio contains every industry in small-cap, mid-cap, and large-cap US companies as well as both international and emerging market companies. The remaining 10 percent of my investments are in those fun things we've discussed: angel investing in companies like Gary's game store, my friend Sean Halle's microchip company, and opportunities I've learned about through my friend Charles Hudson at Precursor Ventures, an angel investor who seeks and supports dozens of new seed fund companies each year. Again, I'm not involved in angel investing to make a huge profit (I typically don't) but so that I can have my finger on the local business pulse. It makes me feel fulfilled to play a role in some of the exciting new businesses in my area.

The "local" part is important. In the Bay Area, a lot of people are inclined to invest more in the tech space because that's what's familiar. If the risk involved doesn't feel worth it, that's fine. The "fun" investment allocation should be just that: fun. If it's not, don't waste your time and energy on it.

A One-Decision Decision

I first moved to the Bay Area in 1994 when I was a twenty-two-year-old student. As with many folks from out of state, the cost of living was a bit of a shock for me. My first job out of grad school, at Dean Witter, paid a salary of $18,000. My next paid about $30,000. I started my own business in 2001, which required making a lot of sacrifices. Plus, as with many entrepreneurs, I encountered some bumps along the way. I was great at opening a lot of new accounts, but I wasn't making much money. For a few years this pattern continued. I wasn't funding my 401K because paying the bills had to come first.

It wasn't until about 2000 when I finally started making enough money to pay off some debts and to really start saving and investing. When I earned my first sizable chunk of money, I used that to pay off most of my student loans, which felt amazing. By the time I left Wall Street I'd had a 401K for just a couple of years, which I liquidated in order to start my own firm. After a good year in 2000, things fell apart for that business. I started over in 2001 with no income and no clients. It wasn't until about 2006 that I was able to really contribute to a 401K, and about the mid-2010s, when I was in my forties, that I was finally making a decent amount of money.

At the end of 2021, I merged my business with another company. When I understood what my buyout would be, I went through three or four iterations of what I could do with that money. As I've mentioned, I am 100 percent invested in equities, so I knew I didn't want to invest in bonds. I reserved some of that money in cash for my emergency fund, and with everything else I had to choose where and how to invest it. For example:

- I could select an actively managed portfolio of mutual funds or ETFs, which would create annual taxation and involve regular rebalancing.
- I could split it between three core funds — one US fund, one diversified international one, and one emerging market fund — rebalancing between them as the various markets performed differently over time.

- Or I could choose a global, all-equity fund that would allow me to own it all in one place.

I went with that third option for two reasons: that fund contains small-, medium-, and large-cap companies, as well as companies from all around the planet, so I won't have to track the transitions and rebalancing. My tax cost is going to be vastly lower for the rest of my life, which is a factor I can control. Performance, on the other hand, I can't control. Nobody knows what any particular investment is going to do, nor any way to accurately predict that.

Something I strongly considered when setting up this fund was its tax cost. The taxes on this fund will be very well managed. It surprises me that most people ignore this issue. It is almost universally true that the more complex — the more moving pieces — your portfolio, the more trading you have to do to maintain your investing process. This, inevitably, leads to more trading costs and higher taxes, both of which are a drag on your long-term performance. It also leads to more "attention" costs — it takes you more time to think about and manage it. I decided at the outset to avoid these costs for myself.

And of course, because I'm my own adviser, I don't pay a fee for that. The only cost I'll have is the internal cost of the fund itself, which is minimal because I chose a low-cost fund. This fund is essentially equivalent to the all-country world index, in that I own all capitalizations and all geographies in one fund. I feel completely comfortable with an all-equities fund and personally don't feel the need for the ballast of bonds.

Aside from the aforementioned global, all-equity fund I set up after my company merger, my accounts are pretty simple:

- **401K:** I was able to start my own 401K about three years into running my own firm, which I've now maxed out, including my contributions and my own company's match.

- **Rollover IRAs:** My wife and I each have a rollover IRA from our previous employers.
- **Roth IRAs:** I make too much money to qualify for a Roth IRA, but I manage both of my children's, which we set up for them and have funded with their earned income since they were each about twelve years old.
- **529 plans:** These are tax-free investment savings accounts specifically meant to be used for college education. My wife and I set 529s up for each of our children when they were about five years old.
- **Health savings account:** This is the only triple-tax-free savings we have access to. The funds will go to cover our healthcare in retirement, but for planning purposes this is the most powerful savings I can commit to because it is a deductible contribution going in, it grows tax-free, and I can use it (subject to some simple limits) tax-free in retirement.
- **Donor-advised fund:** This is a fund that simplifies charitable giving. You initially deposit a chunk of money into it so that over time you have a pool from which you can give to charity (you can continue to add to it or spend it down to zero). You don't have to get receipts or anything because you receive the tax deduction once, at the beginning; whenever you want to give to a certain charity, you just request that the fund donate whatever amount you want.

As I mentioned above, the taxable portfolio is 100 percent invested in a global, all-equity fund that owns fourteen thousand companies of every size, all over the planet, in every industry. It is managed this way for extreme tax efficiency.

Each of the accounts you see listed above is itself tax pro-
tected. I can make rebalancing changes in those accounts without incurring any tax liabilities. In IRAs, 401Ks, 529 plans,
and HSAs, dividends are received tax-free and all transactions
are made tax-free. So there is no tax cost for splitting your
global equity portfolio into, for example, one domestic equity
fund, one developed outside the US fund, and one emerging
market fund. If I rebalance between these funds in a taxable
account, it creates taxable gains. If I rebalance them within
these tax-managed accounts, there are no capital gains.

So instead of investing in those fourteen thousand companies in a single fund, I break them into categories and own the
lowest-cost index in each of the categories. In the equity categories I have broken them down by geography (US, international, emerging markets); capitalization (small, medium, and
large); and growth versus value. Personally, I own a Vanguard
index for growth categories and a Dimensional index for value
categories. One could easily go with all Vanguard or all iShares
or all State Street or all Fidelity or all Dimensional. Once you
are this broadly diversified, the rest of the decisions don't really
add up to much difference in the long term.

This is roughly how my tax-protected investments break
down:

30 percent large-cap US growth
30 percent large-cap US value
5 percent mid-cap US growth
5 percent mid-cap US value
3 percent small-cap US growth
3 percent small-cap US value
9 percent international growth
9 percent international value
6 percent emerging markets

This breakdown roughly approximates the global market-place. The allocations I have lean a little toward the United States but keep a healthy allocation to international markets. People quibble about the specifics. I don't think the allocation specifics matter as much as the consistency of your maintaining the allocations. I feel fantastic about the way my accounts are set up! In fact, if I die before her, my wife won't have to do anything different — other than rebalance. It's essentially a self-managing fund that produces income forever and ever, amen. I call this a one-decision decision. I love not having to put any more energy into it than that. And this is where mindfulness and time come into play again: my number one goal is to be able to do whatever I want with my time. We don't get time back, and that includes the hours we devote to deliberating and stressing out about our portfolios.

Stress, of course, is an inevitable part of life. Things happen, hardships come. But if I don't have to worry about paying attention to my investment accounts and can just let them simmer for years, compounding and growing so that even when I'm gone my family won't have to worry about fussing with them? *That* is a huge payout.

Future Thinking:
How I Envision My Retirement

I am perhaps a bit of a workaholic. I have honestly never considered precisely how I will spend my own retirement. What I mean by that is, I don't envision a time where I will stop working and spend all my time playing *D&D*, traveling, reading, and relaxing. Certainly, there will come a time when I will be doing a lot more of those things, but one of my favorite pastimes *is* my work. I love what I do.

I imagine that as I grow older, I will start discovering new hobbies and pursuing new interests, and then finding a way to turn those hobbies or interests into a business. As I discussed in chapter 13, supporting new businesses is something I love to do. It's exciting to me.

When I begin talking to a client about retirement planning, my first question is "How do *you* define retirement?" We all have our own vision of what it will look like. For me, if retirement means no longer being productive, I'll just never do it. That's not in my nature. If, however, I define retirement as no longer working *for money*? That I could see happening before I turn sixty.

I am a huge believer in education, and particularly in financial education. It's important for me to help people learn about money and how to advance in life. Part of how I've fulfilled this value is by writing a book series, recording podcasts, and creating an online course so that people have access to financial planning even if they aren't ready or able to hire an adviser.

My vision for the future includes creating more group coaching opportunities in my community, both in person and digitally. I could see doing this for both financial literacy and entrepreneurship. I have always loved working with small business owners, so advising them on how to become more successful would be great.

As I've gotten older and seen the advantages my success has offered my kids, I want more and more to work with people who don't have those same advantages. As someone who did not grow up in a house with many resources, I understand what it's like to want. One of the values that's dear to my heart is helping to bridge the wealth gap, both in the Bay Area and beyond. In 2021, I started offering free financial literacy courses in my community, an effort that I will offer more broadly going forward. I also continue to work with programs that support Black and Brown entrepreneurs, provide scholarships for those who are the first in their families to attend college, and support direct reparations. As my "work" time is reduced, I will be adding entrepreneur coaching time.

My investment philosophies are based on my personal value system, coupled with nearly three decades of experience in the game. My three core philosophies remain unwavering: emergency fund first, 90 percent of investable capital in diversified global equities, and 10 percent into something you want to do regardless of whether it pays off.

My biggest guiding principle is time. I can't stress it enough! Time is our most valuable resource. We should be doing anything we can do to allocate more of our time to the things we care about. Before moving on to the conclusion of this book, I thought it'd be fun to look at some of the biggest investment fads and time-wasters out there, which are all founded on one of the most dangerous investment traps there is: speculation.

MINDFUL INVESTING ACTIVITY

In appendix C, I translate how I invest into how you might invest. After all, my investment philosophy and how I follow it are the underpinnings of this book. As we've discussed throughout this book, there's no trick or secret sauce, just diversification, patience, and rebalancing. That's true for both the newbie investor and the financial professional — as you can see from my own examples.

Take the time to review that information. Look at it next to your own portfolio and plans and see how they compare. To reiterate, this is how *I* invest. You have different risk tolerances, different goals, and different life circumstances to consider. It would be presumptuous for any financial adviser to insist that everyone invest as they do. But it is worth giving some thought as to how your plan compares to mine, if only to think about whether the choices you've made are the best for your goals, or if any of them reflect emotional reactions and fears that are holding you back.

CHAPTER 15

Speculating Yesterday, Today, and Tomorrow

He who glories in his luck may be overthrown by destiny.
— EURIPIDES

In 2003, NBC News anchor Brian Williams was in Iraq to cover the US invasion. While there, he flew in a helicopter traveling about an hour behind a trio of US choppers, one of which was shot and had to make an emergency landing. The other two helicopters in that trio were forced to land, and when Williams's craft caught up, an hour or so later, it landed as well. It was no doubt a terrifying experience, particularly as a sandstorm then rolled in, grounding Williams and the crews of all four helicopters in the desert for days. At the time, this is how he reported the story. However, in numerous interviews and blog posts in the coming months and years, his story shifted.*

---

* The Williams saga was covered extensively in the press; see, for example, Paul Farhi, "Brian Williams Admits That His Story of Coming Under Fire while in Iraq Was False," *Washington Post*, February 4, 2015; Pamela Engel, "Brian Williams Explains How He 'Misremembered' the Iraq Helicopter Incident," *Business Insider*, February 9, 2015; Ryan Parker, "Brian Williams Misremembers — and the Internet Won't Let Him Forget It," *Los Angeles Times*, February 5, 2015.

In some tellings, Williams described in detail the American soldiers and the shots that took down the helicopter; he related how the chopper in front of his was hit and how they were all forced down. In other accounts, Williams reported that his own chopper was shot. In yet others, he recalled *seeing* the choppers ahead of his get shot.

Rather than sticking with the first part of the story, in which Williams's chopper was well behind the others and he couldn't have seen the incident, he started to blur the facts and conflate his story with that of the others who witnessed or experienced the shooting. Yes, most of what Williams reported *did* happen, but *how* he reported it shifted. He told stories as if he were there for all of it.

Was Williams merely a skilled liar? It's possible. But what's more likely is that he truly came to believe he *was* in a helicopter that got shot. He wasn't just reporting on the story, he became a part of it. He believed he had seen some of the stuff that happened — the guys on the ground shooting up, the rotor taking an RPG and going down — because he was surrounded by the story and had retold it to himself and the world over and over.

We are all subject to making subconscious revisions to our own stories and to thinking more highly of ourselves than perhaps we deserve. Everyone — including smart people like Brian Williams and you and me — is subject to a mental foible known as fundamental attribution error or correspondence bias. We tend to believe that it's our doing when things go well and not our fault when they don't. When we win, we believe it's due to our work ethic or our own creative genius. When we lose, someone else is to blame — our parents for screwing us up, our lazy coworker for flubbing the project, and so forth. In finance, we want to believe that our outlier wins will continue, and we let them act as team captain when they should really remain on the sidelines.

This thinking is at the heart of the get-rich-quick mindset. We want to believe that when we've done well with some big investment, trusted the right talking head, or gotten in early on a social media fad, that our success was due to our own genius. And being such geniuses, we'll probably keep succeeding. We get to feel good that *we* made the right move. "I *knew* that was a good investment," we say to ourselves. If that investment didn't do so hot and we lost money, we tend to blame environmental factors or other people. And we downplay that loss. No investment broker is shouting to the world about their bad calls. Rather, they point out their wins, and that's the story we believe.

Brian Williams spent years telling his story as if he saw every moment he'd reported on. And it's possible he started to believe that narrative. He could have been so invested in what was happening around him that he took on the entire experience as if he lived through every part of it (even after redacting his story and apologizing on air). Traders tell themselves the same types of narratives. It can be dangerous to place too much credence in the narratives people tell us about how successful they are at trading. The reality is that a whole bunch of academic research supports the contention that most people fail at this kind of practice. When you look at the universe of active management you would think that there would be some consistent high performers, but there really aren't.

Past Performance Is No Guarantee of Future Results

Some managers do well for three years, then poorly for the next five. Then maybe they're good for the next three years, then bad again for another five. And when they're really good, we place all our faith in them because we want to believe it's possible for us to consistently do well too.

A great example of this is what happened with ARK Invest CEO Cathie Wood in 2021. Wood was considered one of the top investors in the country. She literally had the highest performing fund in 2020. Wood did well for a long time. She was interviewed on every program and in every paper. She was widely respected as one of the best investors in all things high tech. People saw her success and chased that money — and a *lot* of people gave Cathie Wood their money to invest. Then, in 2021, Wood was off. Way off. ARK's ETFs dropped by over 40 percent, in a year where the market was up by over 20 percent. Wood lost an enormous amount of her investors' money. How could that happen?

Well, as Wood became more and more successful, she ended up managing hundreds of millions of dollars more than she had before, which meant she was no longer able to manage money in the same way. Managing $50 million is different from managing $500 million. She suddenly had so much money that she could no longer invest in some areas, because when you invest $500 million in a tiny thing you move the market. With $50 million, you could still invest in, say, Microsoft, and that investment wouldn't change the stock's price. But if you invested, say, $5 *billion* in Microsoft, you'd move the price, even though there would still be many other people investing in Microsoft at the same time.

When people saw that Cathie Wood was on top and was making these ridiculous, incredible returns, a whole bunch of people took their money away from other managers and gave it to her instead. She had a whole new structure to manage, and she couldn't adapt fast enough. She didn't have the trading tools and there wasn't enough stuff for her to buy, but she had capital that she still needed to put to work. With that much money in play, she started bidding up the price of the things she was buying, which meant the share prices didn't go up as fast anymore, so people stopped giving her as much to invest. Stocks went up in value because she'd pushed the prices up with her own purchases, but then there was no more money for her to invest, so the climb tapered off. The people who gave her their money saw they'd started to come up short, so they started pulling out, which meant Wood then had to sell that stuff, which pushed down the price again.

This is a normal cycle, built around excitement for a specific subgroup of stocks. At some point, revenues, profits, and dividends reassert their importance. Once one space gets too hot, speculators will find a different space that no one is paying attention to, they'll invest there, and they'll make money.

Cathie Wood's story is indicative of the problem with active management. When we look at the returns of top-performing managers throughout history, no one ever stays on top. Figures 9 and 10 (see next two pages) show two simple examples of this, for both equity and fixed income categories.

In the first graph (figure 9), we see that for actively managed equity funds in a five-year period (June 2012 to June 2017), only 18 percent of top performers stay on top in the next five years (June 2017 to June 2022). For the top quartile of actively managed fixed income funds, just 30 percent stay on top for the following five years.

In the next graph (figure 10), we see an even more granular year-over-year approach. Starting with the top quartile managers as of June 2018, only 41.5 percent are still in the top quartile one year later. By June 2020, just over one-third

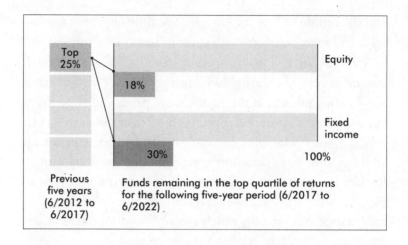

Figure 9. Performance over two nonoverlapping five-year periods shows that top quartile performance does not persist.*

are in the top quartile, and only 4 percent remain on top in June 2021. The decline among bond managers is even faster: 19 percent remain on top in 2019, 3 percent in 2020, and 1.4 percent in June 2021. By midyear 2022, none of the leading equity or bond managers from 2018 are still in the top quartile.

Simply put, this is evidence against the persistence of active performance. A successful manager's investments will be good for a time, until they're not. Recall again the phrase "past performance is no guarantee of future results." Really, past performance has *nothing whatsoever* to do with future results.

In fact, past performance is almost a negative indicator of future results. Even if you're in the top quartile this year,

---

* Source: S&P Dow Jones Indices' US Persistence Scorecard Mid-Year 2022. *Equity* category refers to all domestic funds, which includes large-, medium-, small-, and multi-cap equity funds; *fixed income* refers to all domestic taxable funds in the University of Chicago's Center for Research in Security Prices (CRSP) Survivor-Bias-Free US Mutual Fund Database.

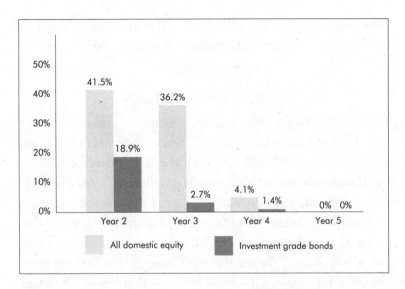

Figure 10. Active manager success persistence over consecutive one-year periods[*]

you're just as likely to be in the bottom quartile next year. You can't bet on anything in the short term. So what do you bet on? Take the "active" out of it and reduce the cost. Your money is still invested (passively), but you won't experience big differences between *your* performance and the markets' performance. Any active management will sometimes lead to outperforming markets and sometimes lead to underperforming markets, and the fee for active management is *always* a drag on net returns. The average performance of all active managers is *lower* than their comparable index (even before they apply their fees). Once we factor in those fees, we are far better off just embracing the index itself and staying broadly diversified. It's not that you won't lose any money and it's not that you're any safer, it's that you're saving your time and improving your

[*]   Source: S&P Dow Jones Indices' US Persistence Scorecard Mid-Year 2022.

compounding by paying lower fees. The advantage is that you get to do it passively and see steady returns.

Too Much Trading

In *Mindful Money* I wrote about how illusions around money reside in our unconscious mind, where they wreak havoc on our emotions. One such illusion is the "get rich quick" idea — a scheme that almost always ends in failure. We tell ourselves stories to justify the possibility of some of these schemes paying off. More often than not, we use examples of people winning to guide our get-rich-quick dreams — not the examples of people losing. We see this with lotto tickets. Are we most likely to lose the two bucks we spent on that Powerball ticket? Yes. But we still buy it because there's a *chance* it will pay off big. We've seen it happen (to other people). An example of this same mindset in the world of investing? Day-trading.

Day traders buy and sell a particular security within the same day. They are betting on a certain stock price to go up, so they buy a bunch of shares in the morning and sell them in the afternoon for (hopefully!) a quick profit. Day traders do this with stocks all day, buying and selling with the intention of making profit based on their guesses about which companies will go up and which will go down. At certain firms, day traders must end every day with liquidity, meaning that all their shares must be sold. With every single trade, you must be right twice: at the entrance *and* at the exit. And being right at both the buy *and* the sell is a big ask. People just can't do that successfully over a long period. And the research agrees.

Day-trading is *not* investing. It is speculating. And it can be fun to speculate and play the day-trading game as long as you're viewing it as entertainment, not as a reliable source of income or consistent returns. The minute people who are speculating start to believe they are investing is the moment they start to fail.

There is no evidence that anyone has been able to predictably outperform the market by day-trading. The act of day-trading means that when you lose, you lose, and when you win, you owe income tax on your winnings. And all the while you are paying the bid-ask spread* and any associated transaction costs. It's hard to justify.

There is an entire subculture that's been built up to gamify day-trading. Robinhood is a fitting example of this. While the company purportedly exists to increase access to trading for folks with less money to play with (its entire structure is built around buying fractional shares, and you can start with as little as one dollar), what most people using the service are doing is playing with their money.

The risk with day-trading is huge. And what's more, it takes up a *lot* of time. I know people who are glued to their monitors buying and selling throughout the day, reading the latest subreddit in search of the next market fad that might cause this stock price to go up or that one to go down, hoping to buy moments before prices go up then sell right before they tilt back down. It's an exhausting game built on speculation.

Remember, speculating and investing are *not* the same thing. *Speculating* means buying something (a stock or real estate, for example) in the hope it will go up in price, preferably quickly, so that you can sell it for a profit. *Investing* means

---

*   The bid-ask spread is the difference between the lowest price a seller is willing to sell a security and the highest price a buyer is willing to pay for the same security. Whenever you trade "at market" you always receive the least advantageous of these two prices. If you buy, you receive the seller's stated price; if you sell, you receive the buyer's stated price. When you trade a lot, you multiply the negative effect on your portfolio.

putting your money, energy, and attention into something with the goal of cultivating steady returns over an extended period. Day traders are speculators, constantly hunting for the next hot stock. They must make quick decisions based on excitement and speed, which often clouds their judgment. Investing your money involves a long-term outlook, like buying and holding a diverse portfolio and letting it grow and build a future cash flow that will keep paying you indefinitely. As mindful investors, we need to constantly return our attention to value, rather than letting our focus drift to price. It's about accumulation, not speculation.

Sector or "Single-Idea" Concentration

In 2021, if you searched online for "investing," you'd find a whole bunch of articles and subreddits about GameStop, Bitcoin, and Tesla. Why? Because that was what other people were searching for. The most talked-about topics in the media are the ones that will stay on top. And because the media is worried about what is trending *now*, searching for "investing" won't lead you to the best investments — it'll just lead you to the hot topics that are getting the most hits. Once something gets more hits, it also gets more attention. The number of people searching for a thing makes that thing rise to the top of the search engine results, which means that even more people will write about it; those articles then show up in searches, keeping that thing popular, in a vicious circle.

What is trending is just trendy; it has nothing to do with whether it's a sound investment. Trending is a function of attention, not quality. This concept is important to understand as you formulate your long-term return expectations. But we tend to focus on areas that we're hearing a lot about — availability bias. Tech is a perfect example of how our psychology creates this problem. As the price of a single company goes up, it attracts attention. If it goes up further, it attracts more attention. The more attention it gets, the more the public's beliefs change. As prices go up, people think that risk is declining and opportunity is increasing; in reality, the excitement and hype are what's driving the price. The stock could very well be a terrible investment opportunity — or at least far less of a secure opportunity than the buzz leads us to believe.

Tech is the largest sector in the economy right now and we should certainly be invested in it. The key is to not overdo it in any single industry. The problem with specific-sector investing is the same as with individual stock investing: concentration creates greater volatility in both directions. Single-company concentration is more extreme than single-sector, but the idea is the same. To use a mixed metaphor here, you should cast a wide net and avoid getting caught up in the headlines like the rest of the sheep. Remember, we should be investing when things are looking *less* great, not when things are getting hyped and their prices driven up. This same concept applies to the rest of today's trending investment tools: meme stocks, crypto, NFTs, and SPACs. Before we talk about those, a word on real estate.

REITs and (Not-So-Passive) Real Estate

By 2000 I was buying about one property per year. When the Great Recession hit in 2008, I owned eighteen units, all in my hometown of Rapid City, South Dakota. I like to call places like Rapid City the bond market of real estate, meaning that while home values aren't going to rise dramatically they'll also stay pretty stable over a long period. For example, in 2002 I bought a four-bedroom house in Rapid City for $140,000. I rented it out for about twelve years. By the time I sold that house in 2014, it was valued at $145,000. You see what I mean about "the bond market of real estate." That house was still a worthwhile investment (the tenants basically paid for the mortgage), I just didn't make a ton of money on it, as I would have in a growing market like Austin or Oakland. In those regions, I would have been able to sell that house for far more than I'd paid for it, so that in addition to the income from rent I'd see a bigger equity return from the value of the house itself.

Overall, I had a nice cash flow from real estate because I got in at the right time and bought inexpensive properties in South Dakota that I hired a local manager to oversee while I remained in California. My first manager was really expensive and, in addition to their management fee, charged a percentage for any work they did on my properties. A few years in, I changed to a new management company that *only* charged a fee, which was a percentage of the monthly rent for each unit, rather than charging for every activity they assisted in.

Aside from the fees, managing these properties — even when I had a management company! — required quite a bit of time. It's unavoidable. Sometimes I felt like the postal service — in rain, in sleet, in snow, on holidays, at nights, on weekends, you just have to take the calls. Generally I only got calls when a repair was going to be over $500, but that time added up. I also had to handle all the paperwork for taxes and reporting. If the city sent a "clean the yard" notice, I had to send it to the management company to take care of. My point is that owning real estate is not a passive investment, even with someone else managing the property.

Owning real estate is like owning a business. Your product is the unit being rented and your income is the rent being paid. You manage costs just like you do in a business, and you increase rents over time to stay profitable. Real estate investing can be a relatively passive activity if it's done via a REIT, or it can be more active (for example, when you're involved in direct ownership, renovations, or development). The idea that directly owned and operated real estate is "passive" is ridiculous. If you own a building (even if you have people managing it, which of course increases the costs), you will still have to answer phone calls on holidays and weekends, you will still have to make decisions about maintenance and repair options, and you may even have to plunge the toilet or mow the yard.

Most small real estate investors disregard the value of their own time in the calculation of returns, which is a huge mistake. You must calculate your own cost into the cost of managing the property: all that time replacing light bulbs, talking to attorneys, finding tenants, or renewing ads. If you don't calculate it into the equation then your returns look higher, but that's because you're not factoring in the real cost of your time. Recall here the phrase "time is money." At the end of the day, the only nonrenewable resource we have is time, right? Therefore it's important to frequently check in and ask yourself what you're trading your time for.

For me, the time was never justified by the income. I could use that time making money more efficiently with my own business or just relaxing with my family. And many of my clients feel the same way. I cannot even *tell* you how many clients have come to me stressed out about their real estate investments and looking for the smoothest way to get out. Real estate investments may sound like a source of passive income, but they're not. The only real source of passive income is long-term, diversified portfolio investments.

Another option for those wanting to dip their toes into the real estate market is investing in a real estate investment trust. A REIT is a company that owns, finances, and oversees income-generating real estate. REITs operate much like mutual funds in that they're made up of a pool of capital from numerous investors, so when an individual investor like you or me buys shares of a REIT, we earn dividends from that fund. The returns on REITs are nowhere near as good as owning real estate directly, but the popularity of REITs has increased over the years because they provide an accessible way for more people to invest in real estate without having to directly buy a property and, well, do anything.

Meme Stocks

The word *meme* has been around a lot longer than many of us think. Its first use is traced back to evolutionary biologist Richard Dawkins, who in his 1976 book *The Selfish Gene* defined a meme as a "unit of cultural transmission," or the cultural equivalent of a gene. As the internet grew from a place where we share information to a place we share stupid jokes, the term took on a whole new meaning. You can't even look at Instagram today without seeing a picture of a cat saying something clever (or stupid).

Memes are *everywhere*. Some are lasting jokes, and some are funny for only a moment. And many are just too ridiculous to make much sense. The thing with memes is that it's impossible to tell which ones will last and which we'll forget about by next week. Memes are unpredictable, and as investments, meme-stock risks are unmanageable.

A meme stock is one that gains popularity via social media. An investor shares a meme about a certain company or trade idea on a platform like Reddit, the meme gains popularity and becomes a brief craze, and people start buying shares of that company because of the enormous amount of attention that meme stock has gotten. Buying meme stocks is *not* investment, it is speculation.

Meme stocks are exciting on the way up, of course! But that upward price change is a function of the excitement, not of the company doing more or better business. The more quickly the price changes, the more it shows up in headlines, the more people are attracted to the meme, the more follow-up headlines appear, the more buyers step in to support the price and push it upward, and voilà, you have a GameStop situation.

Virtually no one who engages with any meme stock cares about the underlying business or commodity and its place in the world. They are buying the meme, not the investment itself. They are buying the emotion, heedless of revenue, profits, or dividends.

Meme stocks are not a path to wealth or financial freedom. They are distractions that keep you trapped in a market-focused and performance-driven world.

Cryptocurrencies

As of April 2023, CoinMarketCap reports there are over 23,000 cryptocurrencies trading on 611 exchanges with a value of roughly $1.3 trillion.* The most talked about is still Bitcoin, but there are many new digital assets on the market. In an increasingly digitized world, people like the idea of a decentralized digital currency that is transferred between peers rather than a central authority.

Crypto is still very new. And it may very well be the next big thing, but whether Bitcoin is trading at $47,000 (as it was on March 30, 2022), $15,782 (November 21, 2022), or $30,320 (April 16, 2023), it's still too early to know. There

---

* See "All Cryptocurrencies," CoinMarketCap.com, n.d.

have been many crypto promises that have already been broken, such as its value as a stable currency, a medium of exchange, a source of anonymity, or a hedge against inflation. Even if we get broad adoption at this point, I don't know what problem crypto (as a currency) solves.

Something that always gives me pause is the "coolness" factor of the thing: people *like* to own Bitcoin, and they *love* to say they own it. Or for some, Bitcoin is old school, and some new alt coin is the cutting edge. The thing is that it's all speculation at this point. Crypto acceptance, familiarity, conversance, and ownership are important signals to the community about your hipness as an investor. The lack of the same is an equally important signal.

I'm absolutely not saying don't buy cryptocurrency (or any of the investments in this chapter). What I'm saying is make sure it is part of the right segment of your investments. Go back and review chapter 14 — if 90 percent of your investments are safely tucked into diversified global equity funds (ballasted with bonds if you must) and you're not pulling from those to feed your crypto craving (and you're not hoping your crypto bets will pay off your mortgage), by all means go for it. If you are using that 10 percent of your holdings to play with something that interests you, that's great. But it is speculation. You must be willing to lose that 10 percent. No one knows where crypto will end up. If it does turn out to be an important investment category in the future, no one can reliably predict which coins will come out on top. And even if specific coins dominate, no one can tell today what path they will take to get there.

You don't have to invest directly in crypto to gain the benefits of crypto. If you are invested in the great businesses of the United States and the rest of the world and crypto *does* become a thing, then those businesses you've invested in will start utilizing crypto and you'll see its benefits in that way. By investing in businesses you are exposed to the crypto winners, without speculating on which cryptocurrency or trending *thing* will do well. Investing in businesses means never having to worry about not being a part of it. This goes for every new and shiny thing... not just crypto.

Maybe the technology works out the way they say it will, but there's no reason to think that it will any more than there is a reason to think that it won't. As of yet, there's no meat there. Without the proof, it's difficult for me to call it a great investment. Crypto is filled with a whole lot of guessing right now. Some people have been and will be very lucky with their guesses. I, however, will not base my financial future on guesswork or hope.

NFTs? SPACs?

I'm just going to say it: NFTs baffle me. Non-fungible tokens are digital assets that anyone can have a copy of, but that enable one person to claim ownership of. Think of it like this: millions of people own prints of Van Gogh's *Starry Night*, but there can only ever be one original painting made by the artist himself, with his very own brushes, paint, and canvas. Having an original Van Gogh on your wall would be a powerful thing. Having a digital original of a $69 million Beeple NFT[*] or an $11.75 million CryptoPunk NFT[†] on your screen is a different type of bragging rights. I personally don't see the appeal in being the original owner when I can Google, view, and

---

[*]   "Beeple: A Visionary Digital Artist at the Forefront of NFTs," Christie's, n.d.

[†]   Abby Schultz, "'Covid Alien' CryptoPunk Sells for $11.75 million in Sotheby's Sale," *Barron's*, June 10, 2021.

screengrab almost any NFT out there, but hey, they could be the next big thing.

Of course, there are many potential use cases for NFTs beyond art. They may be used to establish an "in group." In other words, people may one day identify with a certain NFT online; they could be used to demarcate club membership or status levels. But there are a lot of hurdles on the path toward broad adoption of useful NFT technologies. Like crypto, NFTs could totally be a game changer. And they may not be. No one knows at this point. This is what speculation is all about.

Then you have special purpose acquisition companies (SPACs). These are shell companies with no commercial operations. A SPAC is formed for the sole purpose of raising capital through an initial public offering (IPO) in order to buy or merge with an existing company, which then becomes a public company without having to go through the traditional IPO process. The sponsors who create the SPAC intend to use the funds they raise to acquire a company within a specified period, typically two years. Nevertheless, many SPACs never consummate a deal. Money is returned with interest, but there may well have been more productive uses for those funds in the meantime. And the money returned is rarely equal to what went in, since sponsors generally take 20 percent of receipts even when their own investment is minimal. The return on investment on a SPAC depends on factors like the company chosen for acquisition and its market performance. As you can see, there is a lot of room for, shall we say, fishiness.

SPACs and NFTs are both investments that may attract questionable actors hoping to take advantage of market hype (and the people who are attracted by that hype). In fact, the financial press has generated a whole lot of excitement over the sudden increase in SPACs and the advent of NFTs. Between the large sums of money being showered on both, the memes making fun of them, and the involvement of "influencer financiers," there is a lot of buzz. Where there's buzzing, there are flies, and you know where flies like to congregate.

The Good Enough Goal

The meme-stock investing craze we saw in 2021, particularly with GameStop, was interesting. For that four- or five-month period where everything went crazy, the fundamental value of the company failed to be recognized in the market because of the coordinated efforts of a group of investors. A decision to do so was made publicly on a subreddit, resulting in the consensus that, essentially, "Okay guys, we're going to distort this market price." Such activity gets really close to being illegal.

If we were to all get in a private room together and say, "Here's the plan, we're going to collectively borrow a bunch of money and sell all these stocks and push the price down," that would be colluding, which is against the law. You can't do that! That's manipulation. But if a bunch of people are just talking on social media and no one is forcing anyone to do anything; if they're all in agreement but there's no handshake, contract, or requirement that they follow the plan and they know they can get out anytime, it's not illegal. It's just risky and stupid.

Some people made a bunch of money on GameStop and most lost a bunch. It's rare for market efficiency to fail in that way. When it does then something nefarious is probably happening. Stock prices are typically determined by shareholder votes. If more people buy, the price goes up; if more people sell, the price goes down. That's the market, and it's a pretty good mechanism that prices shares at close to what their value should be.

If you trust the market, you don't have to think about all the other stuff.

The thing with speculation and all these new investing trends is that you must pay close and constant attention. And even when you do, the risk is much higher than if you just trusted the traditional market. Set up your diversified funds and let them cook for twenty, thirty, forty years if you can. Sure, you might miss the potential for some really high gains if you had got in at just the perfect moment with the right trending meme stock, but chances are you wouldn't have. The benefit to tuning out the noise is that you get to focus on stuff like, What should my next painting look like? What book will I read next? Where do I want to take my kids on vacation?

I'm suggesting that you will do well enough with a "good enough" plan. There is no "best" investment plan; the more you search for "best," or for any form of optimization, the greater your risk of not even reaching "good enough." Your plan is good enough when you have adequate savings committed to a diversified portfolio of global equities to create a historically average performance (over long periods of time) that will grow your portfolio to a size that will spin off a rising income at a pace that will at *least* keep up with your rising cost of living throughout retirement and beyond. Your performance will be similar to that of your peers. But the "outperformance" you can look forward to will come in the form of recaptured time as you get to ignore the speculations and worries.

The goal is to eventually have the freedom to do whatever you want with your time, right? Remember this: investing is simple. The most important choice you can make for your financial future is to stop predicting, start planning, and stay mindful so your investments last your lifetime.

MINDFUL INVESTING ACTIVITY

Here's another simple practice, and one that won't be much of a surprise if you've read up to this page! If you're intrigued by any form of speculation (as compared to investing), my general rule is to avoid the impulse to get involved. If, however, you have money to (potentially) burn and this is the "fun" thing you want to add to your portfolio, first ask yourself these questions:

- Is your emergency fund in good shape?
- Have you carefully reviewed how much you'll need to have saved for retirement and not just made but implemented a plan to get there?
- To that end, do you already have an investment portfolio that will return enough in the long term to fulfill your planning goals?
- Do you have the time to follow whatever it is you're speculating on and the knowledge to understand the gamble?
- Is this really what you want to do with your "mad money," or is there something else you'd prefer to risk it on? (say, angel investing, or playing the ponies at Belmont,* or just increased spending)?

---

*   Not a recommendation!

Conclusion

It is by his freedom that a man knows himself,
by his sovereignty over his own life
that a man measures himself.
— ELIE WIESEL

There's a saying I love that goes "You're the protagonist in your own story." That is, you are the one your story is written about, and as the author of your story *you* get to make the choices about what happens to you. If you don't make your own choices, the world will make them for you.

The goal as I see it is to have the freedom to do what you want with your time. For many of us, that includes not having to do what other people tell us to. The problem is that a lot of us don't end up making financial decisions that align with our goals. We spend for what we want today and we rely on luck (winning the lottery, receiving an inheritance or valuable company stock, or some other factor outside our control) for tomorrow. In search of the optimal, we miss the good enough. In chapter 8, verse 8 of the *Analects* Confucius said, "Simplicity in one's way of life is not a matter for shame. It is better than elegance and luxury." We spend a lot of time and energy making the process so complicated that we either get swept up in the hype or don't invest at all. Both are huge mistakes.

Starting at first principles and keeping it simple can pay the greatest dividends.

The good news is that investing is incredibly simple. It starts with mindfulness. The mindfulness exercise in chapter 2 asks that you look inward and understand what gives your life meaning — what is your Big Why? What makes you the happiest? What are some of your life goals? Do you want to write a book? Do you want to start your own business? Do you want to switch career paths and pursue something completely different from what you've been doing for the past twenty years? How do you envision your retirement? And a pair of questions a lot of us don't ask ourselves: Where do you see your limiting beliefs sneaking in? And how can you set those aside? We all have limiting beliefs that tell us things like "It's too late in life to make a career shift"; "It'll be too hard to start my dream business"; "Writing a book is not something I could ever do"; "There's no way I could ever retire before I turn seventy."

The most important thing you can do to achieve your personal and financial goals is to create a written financial plan and stick to it. Once you know what the life you want looks like, you can begin taking concrete steps to realize your vision. Your plan becomes a map that will guide you toward your goal even when obstacles arise — and they will. Your partner could lose their job, your child might get injured, you may get divorced or lose a family member. When those inevitable life events happen, it can be easy to give up on your long-term dreams. But if you have your life map, you can mindfully return your focus to that plan and let it guide you back on course.

Any financial plan starts with consistent saving. If you've already got that going by the time you make a plan, you're a step ahead. But if you don't have consistent, increasing savings, you will not make it. That is the base minimum. "Save, save, save!" as my mother always says. Then once you have consistent, increasing savings, you must invest and then mindfully stay the course.

Some mindful reminders to leave you with:

- Understand what makes you happy and make a plan.
- Save consistently. Fund your emergency fund first, so those inevitable emergencies won't throw you off course.
- Invest simply. Don't listen to the social media hype.
- A long-term outlook is key. The goal is not to be a day trader, a week trader, or a month trader. We should be setting up our accounts for the distant future: twenty, thirty, forty years if we can. If we want to enjoy greater returns, we must accept the zigs and the zags and remember that the overall movement of the market is up.
- Be mindful that short-term volatility is totally normal, and that risk and volatility are not the same thing. Markets are unpredictable and we tend to overreact to the headlines. A nonjudgmental awareness of volatility begins with a trust in the future recovery of markets.
- Remember the evidence. Markets are durable, headlines aren't helpful, and volatility is not the same thing as risk. When you are mindfully aware that markets will zig and zag, you can hold on to your investments and not worry. The markets have always recovered in the past and there's no reason to believe that they won't do so again the next time they drop.
- Be mindful of the limitations of your knowledge. Much as we must acknowledge and push aside our limiting beliefs, we also need to understand and accept

the limitations of our knowledge when it comes to investing. In other words, we cannot know the future. No one can consistently predict which specific stock is going to win or lose, so we shouldn't even bother trying. By sticking mindfully to our appropriately asset-allocated and broadly diversified investment funds, in the long term we will see much steadier results.

Investing is simple. It is also boring. But do you really want to be that person glued to your computer screen, scanning headlines for the next get-rich-quick stock? It's true that if you stick with a diversified, global portfolio that you rebalance annually, you will not see crazy high wins, but you probably won't see enormous losses either. What you'll see is steady, long-term growth. But that will only happen if you start by determining what you want, understanding how simple investing really is, and remaining mindful. Stop predicting, start planning, and stay mindful. Remember, you are the protagonist in your story, and you get to decide how your story will play out.

Acknowledgments

I can't express gratitude without repeating myself a little from my first book. My parents are still terrific — Mom is grounded and practical, while Dad continues to dream of how things should be better than they are. My wife is still a devoted mom and a wonderful friend. My kids remain my inspiration. It is my honor to share this leg of our journey together.

My Berkeley EP Wealth team — Scott Jacobs, Gail Lieberman, John Madden, and Carrie Sax — you are still tireless in your advocacy for and dedication to our clients. I could not have kept Mindful Money together in late 2021 or completed the transition to EP Wealth without your strength.

Thank you to my Mindful Money team — Nicole Williams, for helping me manage our courses and for continually rebuilding our website and member communications; Harry Duran, for helping me launch and manage the *Mindful Money* podcast; and Jon Schumacher, for helping me create our free webinar and the Financial Freedom Workshop. You are helping me fulfill the dream I had with my brother of helping people who don't have access to financial advice with mindful financial education and coaching.

I'd like to thank the majority of the financial commentariat for their dependable overconfidence and bias blindness. The punditry I have listened to for three decades have shown themselves, time and again, to be wrong more often than they are right. I especially appreciate errors so obviously and spectacularly wrong as to give me fodder for my own "no-prediction zone" commentary. If it were not for their stalwart consistency, I would never have the courage to write such a book.

I'd also like to thank Josh Brown, Ben Carlson, Jonathan Clements, Meb Faber, Howard Lindzon, Wade Pfau, Cullen Roche, J. D. Roth, Bob Seawright, Jason Zweig, Mr. Money Mustache, the Financial Samurai, and the Bogleheads for not getting distracted by the many and varied shiny objects that get presented in the financial advisory and F.I.R.E. space. You all lead the way ... if only we would listen.

The last couple of years have been a personal struggle, and I am grateful to everyone who has offered an ear, a shoulder, or a kind word. In June of 2021 my brother, David DeYoe, died. I cannot describe what this did to me. It changed everything. The ground slipped out from under me. I never would have completed this project were it not for the following folks.

Shane Grajczyk "Cuz," thanks for dropping everything and coming out. It meant the world to me that you were here both to distract me a little and to help me see what was real when I lost the thread.

John Faxio, thank you for our daily walks for those many months. Thank you for meeting me at my front door. Thank you for walking silently, for listening to me blather, for hearing my anger without judgment, and for offering a thought or a perspective when it would help.

Jason Steinberg, thank you for sharing the memories with me. Thank you for the stories. Thanks for reminding me of both how brilliant and how stupid Dave could be. Thanks for the opportunity to laugh amid so many tears.

Lisa Caplan, thank you for all your hearts. Thank you for stating clearly that I don't need to respond. Thank you for sticking with it. You are an angel.

Jay Gunther, Gary Ray, and Chris Williams (my men), thank you for listening completely, encouraging me to get it out, and commenting softly. It is a blessing to have three men who can share as deeply as we have shared. It is an even greater blessing to know that you all knew Dave as well.

Kaira Jewel Lingo and Susie Harrington, thank you for giving me the tools to overcome emotional overwhelm and resume my daily meditation practice.

Mariah Bear, thank you for working with me to complete the manuscript, rework everything, and complete the editing before turning it over to the New World Library team. I look forward to working with you on the next one as well.

Georgia Hughes, Monique Muhlenkamp, and Kristen Cashman (and all the folks at New World Library), thanks for working with me to get this second book out into the world. I so enjoyed the process of the first one, and the final product was better than I could have hoped for. It has been a pleasure to work with you all once again.

How Do I Begin Investing?

A (Relatively) Simple Flowchart

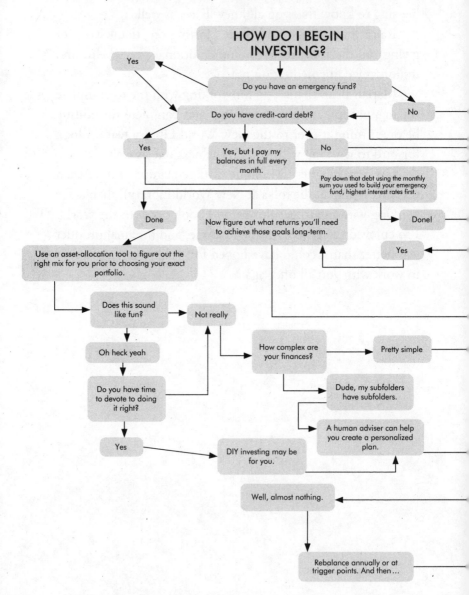

HOW DO I BEGIN INVESTING?

Do you have an emergency fund?

Yes

No

Do you have credit-card debt?

Yes

Yes, but I pay my balances in full every month.

No

Pay down that debt using the monthly sum you used to build your emergency fund, highest interest rates first.

Done

Now figure out what returns you'll need to achieve those goals long-term.

Done!

Yes

Use an asset-allocation tool to figure out the right mix for you prior to choosing your exact portfolio.

Does this sound like fun?

Not really

Oh heck yeah

How complex are your finances?

Pretty simple

Do you have time to devote to doing it right?

Dude, my subfolders have subfolders.

A human adviser can help you create a personalized plan.

Yes

DIY investing may be for you.

Well, almost nothing.

Rebalance annually or at trigger points. And then…

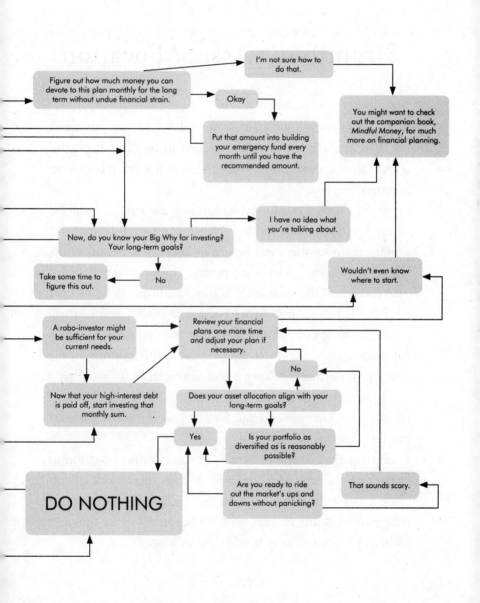

Figure out how much money you can devote to this plan monthly for the long term without undue financial strain.

I'm not sure how to do that.

Okay

You might want to check out the companion book, *Mindful Money*, for much more on financial planning.

Put that amount into building your emergency fund every month until you have the recommended amount.

Now, do you know your Big Why for investing? Your long-term goals?

I have no idea what you're talking about.

No

Take some time to figure this out.

Wouldn't even know where to start.

A robo-investor might be sufficient for your current needs.

Review your financial plans one more time and adjust your plan if necessary.

No

Now that your high-interest debt is paid off, start investing that monthly sum.

Does your asset allocation align with your long-term goals?

Yes

Is your portfolio as diversified as is reasonably possible?

DO NOTHING

Are you ready to ride out the market's ups and downs without panicking?

That sounds scary.

APPENDIX B

Simplifying Asset Allocation

W hile the philosophy of portfolio management won't change at all, how you choose to build your portfolio will have a direct impact on how much work rebalancing becomes.

In the simplest portfolio, there are only three items — global all-cap equities, bonds, and cash. When you are rebalancing this simple portfolio, there will be less to keep track of and to do. Of course, you can go with 100 percent equities and reduce this even further — the trade-off is higher volatility.

Even if you entirely avoid individual stocks, you can still create an equity portfolio using indices that has eighteen different holdings with little overlap (see the fourth column on the next page). Rebalancing such a portfolio is far more complex.

The graphic on the next page shows the difference between the simplest portfolio on the far left and the most complex portfolio on the far right.

Personally, I like to keep my portfolio in the two columns farthest to the left. Most advisers will do their work in columns 4 and 5. Evidence suggests there is little long-term portfolio value to doing so. I see no reason to stray toward the right and every reason to keep it as simple as possible.

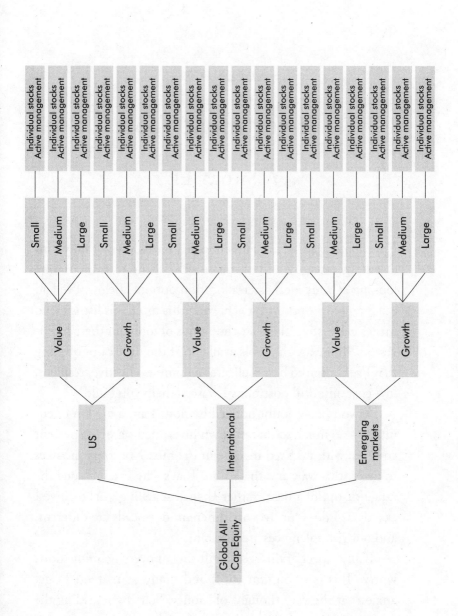

APPENDIX C

Investment Tools

A SHORT LIST

In chapter 14, I give a fairly detailed breakdown of how I invest, by category, and of course we've spent a fair bit of time looking at your ideal asset-allocation options. Below, I've laid out a range of options for achieving this mix. This list is by no means exhaustive; there are thousands of tools out there for investors. These are the tools available at the time of publishing that I've chosen to best replicate the simple, effective, resilient, low-cost, mindful portfolios I want to help you build.

As you've no doubt noticed by now, I am a big fan of equities — so much so that my own investments are 100 percent equities, with no fixed income in the mix. Not everyone likes to invest this way, and that's fine! That's why I've included the range of options here, rather than just telling you to invest exactly as I do. Our lives are different, our needs are different, and our risk tolerances are different.

If any aspect of this feels confusing or overwhelming, don't worry. This is important stuff, and many of us tend to get anxious at the very thought of money. Start by rereading the relevant section of the book and, if you're still unsure, it may be time to consult a financial professional (using, of course, the hints for finding the right one in chapter 7).

When I say "own everything!" it's just about that simple. I break the total investment portfolio into categories, and I own the lowest-cost index in each of the categories. Personally, I have broken the equity categories down across many distinct variables:

1. Geography (US, international, emerging markets)
2. Capitalization (small, medium, and large)
3. Growth versus value

I own a variety of Vanguard indices across the growth categories and a variety of Dimensional funds for value categories. This decision isn't all that important; one could easily go all-in with Vanguard, iShares, State Street, Fidelity, or Dimensional, or mix and match as desired. The important thing is to establish the right asset allocation and get broadly diversified. Once you do so, the rest of the decisions don't really make much difference in the long term.

For purposes of greater simplicity, below I have simplified this even further by merging growth, value, small, medium, and large companies into a single index tool based on geography.

The equity portion of my tax-protected investments (again, see chapter 14) can be simplified as follows:

76 percent US equity
18 percent international equity
6 percent emerging markets equity

If you choose to have 0 percent exposure to bonds, then this is an excellent starting point for your own portfolio. If you wish to include bonds to dampen volatility, then the following chart is your starting point. Pick your column based on exactly how much volatility you wish to offset. More bonds mean less volatility. Remember, more bonds also mean lower long-term returns. Pick your trade-off wisely.

	Conser-vative	Income	Balanced	Growth	Aggres-sive
BONDS	80%	60%	40%	20%	0%
US EQUITY	15%	30%	45%	61%	76%
INT'L EQUITY	4%	8%	11%	14%	18%
EMERGING MARKET EQUITY	1%	2%	4%	5%	6%

Alternatively, if even this seems too complex, you can select one of the global, all-equity investments to simplify the process even further (see next page). This is how I invest my taxable portfolio in its entirety.

Here are tools to consider that fit the low-cost, index-based model we've been discussing, including current fees and returns, broken down by broad category of investment.

Global, All Equity

These investments provide a way to own small slices of widely diverse companies of all sizes across all industries and all geographies.

COMPANY	SYMBOL	NAME	EXPENSE	YIELD
Vanguard	VT	Vanguard Total World Stock ETF	0.07%	2.09%
Vanguard	VTWAX	Vanguard Total World Stock Market Index Admiral	0.07%	2.06%
State Street	SPGM	SPDR Portfolio MSCI Global Stock Market ETF	0.09%	2.21%
DFA	DGEIX	DFA Global Equity Portfolio	0.25%	1.85%
iShares	ACWI	iShares MSCI ACWI (All Country World Index) ETF	0.32%	1.66%

US Equity

COMPANY	SYMBOL	NAME	EXPENSE	YIELD
Fidelity	FZROX	Fidelity Zero Total Market Index	0.00%	1.45%
State Street	SPTM	SPDR Portfolio S&P 1500 Composite Stock Market ETF	0.03%	1.59%
Vanguard	VTI	Vanguard Total Stock Market ETF	0.03%	1.57%
iShares	ITOT	iShares Core S&P Total US Stock Market ETF	0.03%	1.56%
Vanguard	VTSAX	Vanguard Total Stock Market Index Admiral Shares	0.03%	1.56%
Schwab	SCHB	Schwab US Broad Market	0.03%	1.55%
DFA	DFUS	DFA US Equity ETF	0.09%	1.41%
DFA	DFEOX	DFA US Equity Core 1	0.14%	1.47%
iShares	ESGU	iShares ESG MSCI USA ETF	0.15%	1.62%
DFA	DFSIX	DFA US Sustainability Core 1 Portfolio	0.17%	1.33%

International Equity

COMPANY	SYMBOL	NAME	EXPENSE	YIELD
Fidelity	FZILX	Fidelity Zero International Index Fund	0.00%	2.57%
State Street	SPDW	SPDR Portfolio Developed World ex-US ETF	0.04%	2.94%
Vanguard	VEA	Vanguard FTSE Developed Markets ETF (ex US)	0.05%	2.91%
Vanguard	VTMGX	Vanguard Developed Markets (ex US) Index	0.05%	2.89%
Schwab	SCHF	Schwab International Equity ETF (Large Blend)	0.06%	2.63%
iShares	IXUS	iShares Core MSCI Total International Stock ETF	0.07%	2.36%
Schwab	SCHC	Schwab International Small-Cap Equity ETF	0.11%	1.72%
DFA	DFAI	DFA International Core Equity ETF	0.18%	2.65%
iShares	ESGD	iShares ESG MSCI EAFE ETF	0.20%	2.4%
DFA	DFIEX	DFA Core International Equity Portfolio	0.24%	2.76%
DFA	DFSPX	DFA International Sustainability Core 1	0.25%	2.13%

Emerging Markets

COMPANY	SYMBOL	NAME	EXPENSE	YIELD
Vanguard	VWO	Vanguard FTSE EM	0.08%	3.83%
Vanguard	VEMAX	Vanguard EM Index Admiral Shares	0.08%	3.77%
Fidelity	FPADX	Fidelity EM Index	0.08%	2.44%
iShares	IEMG	iShares Core MSCI EM	0.09%	2.65%
State Street	SPEM	SPDR Portfolios EM	0.11%	3.35%
Schwab	SCHE	Schwab EM Equity	0.11%	2.87%
iShares	ESGE	iShares ESG MSCI EM	0.25%	2.64%
DFA	DFAE	DFA EM Core Equity ETF	0.35%	2.66
DFA	DFCEX	DFA Core 1 EM	0.40%	3.63%
DFA	DESIX	DFA EM Sustainability Core 1	0.45%	2.41%

Fixed Income

COMPANY	SYMBOL	NAME	EXPENSE	YIELD
State Street	SPAB	SPDR Portfolio Aggregate Bond ETF	0.03%	2.80%
Schwab	SCHZ	Schwab US Aggregate Bond	0.03%	2.78%
Vanguard	VBTLX	Vanguard Total Bond Market Index Admiral Shares	0.03%	2.75%
Vanguard	BND	Total Bond Market ETF	0.03%	2.69%
iShares	AGG	iShares Core US Aggregate Bond ETF	0.03%	2.67%
Fidelity	FXNAX	Fidelity US Bond Index Fund	0.03%	2.63%
Vanguard	VTEAX	Vanguard Intermediate Term National Muni	0.05%	2.46%
Vanguard	VTEB	Tax-Exempt Bond ETF	0.05%	2.41%
Vanguard	VTABX	Vanguard Total International Bond Index Admiral	0.07%	1.71%
iShares	EAGG	iShares ESG US Aggregate Bond	0.10%	2.52%
DFA	DFAPX	DFA Investment Grade Portfolio	0.19%	2.65%
DFA	DGSFX	DFA Global Sustainable Fixed Income	0.23%	1.9%
Fidelity	FBND	Fidelity Total Bond ETF	0.36%	3.72%

Costs and yields were updated as of June 2023, but they can change. Before investing in these or any other investment tools, be sure to verify the given information and learn about what you are buying. All investing involves risk, including the loss of principal. The author is not making any recommendation for any particular investor and takes no liability for the choices people make upon reading the book. Investing means embracing the risks associated with investing. Investing yourself means taking on the risks of investing yourself.

Index

Page references followed by an italicized *fig.* indicate illustrations or material contained in their captions.

Complete Disclaimer

The material in this book is intended for educational purposes only. No expressed or implied guarantee of the effects of the recommendations can be given nor liability taken. All opinions expressed are subject to change without notice, are not intended as investment advice, and are in no sense a prediction of future events. There can be no guarantee that strategies promoted will be successful. All indices referenced are unmanaged and do not reflect fees or expenses. You cannot invest directly in an index, and index performance is not indicative of any particular investment. Past performance does not guarantee future results. All investing involves risk, including loss of principal.

The S&P 500 Index is widely regarded as the best single gauge of the US equities market. The index includes a representative sample of five hundred leading companies in leading industries of the US economy. The S&P 500 Index focuses on the large-cap segment of the market; however, since it includes a significant portion of the total value of the market, it also represents the market.

The price of equity securities may rise or fall, because of changes in the broad market or changes in a company's financial condition, sometimes rapidly and unpredictably. These price movements may result from factors affecting individual companies, sectors, or industries, or the securities market as a whole, such as changes in economic or political conditions. Equity securities are subject to "stock market risk," meaning that stock prices in general may decline over short or extended periods of time.

The JPM Market Insights program provides comprehensive data and commentary on global markets without reference to products. Designed as a tool to help clients understand the markets and support investment decision-making, the program explores the implications of current economic data and changing market conditions.

For the purposes of MiFID II, the JPM Market Insights and Portfolio Insights programs are marketing communications and are not in scope for any MiFID II / MiFIR requirements specifically related to investment research. Furthermore, the J.P. Morgan Asset Management Market Insights and Portfolio Insights programs, as nonindependent research, have not been prepared in accordance with legal requirements designed to promote the independence of investment research, nor are they subject to any prohibition on dealing ahead of investment research.

About the Author

Jonathan K. DeYoe, AIF, is senior vice president and partner at EP Wealth Advisors. He is a Lutheran seminarian turned Buddhist academic turned financial adviser and educator. The bestselling author of *Mindful Money: Simple Practices for Reaching Your Financial Goals and Increasing Your Happiness Dividend*, he is also the founder of Mindful Money — a financial education company. He writes about the intersection of money and happiness in the *Mindful Money Weekly* newsletter and on the *Mindful Money* blog and hosts the *Mindful Money* podcast. Jonathan has helped clients protect, grow, and transfer their wealth for nearly three decades. Through Mindful Money he is focused on supporting wealth creation for folks who don't meet traditional adviser minimums. Jonathan lives in California's Berkeley Hills with his wife of twenty years, two incredible kids, and their fluffy cat Posey.

https://Mindful.Money